Tales of Kentucky Ghosts

Tales of Kentucky Ghosts

WILLIAM LYNWOOD MONTELL

THE UNIVERSITY PRESS OF KENTUCKY

Scholarly publisher for the Commonwealth,
serving Bellarmine University, Berea College, Centre College
of Kentucky, Eastern Kentucky University, The Filson Historical Society,
Georgetown College, Kentucky Historical Society, Kentucky State University,
Morehead State University, Murray State University, Northern Kentucky University,
Transylvania University, University of Kentucky, University of Louisville, and
Western Kentucky University.

Editorial and Sales Offices: The University Press of Kentucky
663 South Limestone Street, Lexington, Kentucky 40508-4008
www.kentuckypress.com

The Library of Congress has cataloged the hardcover edition as follows:

Montell, William Lynwood, 1931-
  Tales of Kentucky ghosts / William Lynwood Montell.
    p. cm.
  Includes bibliographical references and index.
  ISBN 978-0-8131-2593-0 (hardcover : alk. paper)
  1. Ghosts—Kentucky. I. Title.
  BF1472.U6M6625 2010
  133.109769—dc22   2010020653

ISBN 978-0-8131-6827-2 (pbk. : alk paper)
ISBN 978-0-8131-7387-0 (pdf)
ISBN 978-0-8131-3948-7 (epub)

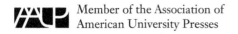 Member of the Association of
American University Presses

In memory of my parents, Willie and Hazel Montell, and my grandfather, Chris Chapman, all of whom were master storytellers; and to my wife, Linda; her daughter, Lisa, and my children, Monisa and Brad, and their progeny; and to all Kentuckians whose devoted interest in storytelling across the years made this book possible.

CONTENTS

Introduction

After enjoying my earlier collections of Kentucky ghost stories, numerous readers pleaded for more. I therefore began gathering additional tales in 2007 by driving around the state, making telephone requests, and contacting staff members at college and university archives. The oral stories recorded for this book, gathered from numerous counties across Kentucky, are all new.

In earlier times, these interesting, sometimes scary, accounts were known as "ghost tales." Some residents, especially in western Kentucky, called them "scary stories," and others simply called them "haunt tales," "haint tales," or "ghost tales." Back then, tale telling was a common social activity on Saturday nights and Sunday afternoons. Young kids sat around, especially at night, to hear what they considered to be realistic accounts. They would get so scared they would jump out of their chairs, or hop up off the floor, run to their beds, and cover themselves with quilts. Sometimes they might even wet the bed if they were too afraid to get out of bed to go to the bathroom or to run outside.

The stories in this book are intricately tied to the critical element of belief in the supernatural, which is typically motivated by hearing an account of the event from a friend or relative. People in all walks of life and in all world cultures cling to their beliefs in the supernatural and to stories about paranormal experiences. Typically, people are not inclined to believe written accounts, but, told orally, these stories gain a power and felt veracity that are hard to dismiss. Folklorists generally agree that such terms as "belief" and "belief tales" should be used to describe the types of supernatural occurrences described in this volume.

As I have advised in previous books, readers should adopt an open mind and an understanding, tolerant attitude toward those who believe they have personally encountered a ghost as an unexplained phenomenon. Many reputed mysteries and occurrences cannot be explained away by scientific means, even in today's advanced world of technology. However, people are often unwilling to believe in the paranormal, regardless of who the storyteller is, because they fear being judged or intimidated by disbelievers.[1] Virtually every story in this book is told as an event that really happened. Thus, it is hard to prove or disprove what is described as an actual encounter with a ghost or ghosts.

Some of the ghost stories included in this book provide historical content: they describe beliefs and practices now remembered only by the older generation. Recording the stories helps to preserve the historical and personal information for future generations. It is sad to think that many strange and interesting stories will be lost because those familiar with the incidents choose to keep them secret for personal reasons.[2]

Some of the stories in this book were told by individuals who firmly believe they have encountered—through sound, sight, or feeling—the disembodied spirit of a deceased person or animal that has materialized by some means unknown to them. The deceased may be a friend, a family member, or a distant relative. It is hard for listeners to question the validity of stories that are told by people they love and respect.[3]

While some ghosts are reputedly sinister and frightening, most are not. Ghosts, as described in told-to-be-true oral narratives, are typically not hostile. They generally appear to be indifferent to the living; some of them are seemingly timid and easily deterred. Most ghosts go about their business in a very unpretentious manner and appear not to want any fanfare. They seem to have a role to perform. If it can be accomplished without contact with living persons, ghosts apparently are quite content to remain unseen.[4]

Tale swapping is a dynamic process in family and other intimate small groups. There is a constant give and take, even by those who do not engage in the storytelling. The constant eye contact and the listeners' uneasy shifting reaffirm belief and intensify the group communication process. Individual narrative art is rewarded by the oohs and aahs and the occasional groans, shudders, and even shrieks from the audience when a performer has finished the tale.[5]

Gathering stories for *Tales of Kentucky Ghosts* was a difficult process, as most of the old-time storytellers are now gone. The parents and grandparents of present-day parents and grandparents were crucial in conveying stories, especially family history accounts, to their progeny. Regrettably, television and other forms of electronic transmission have pushed aside interest in listening to tales and learning about older times. People whose grandparents and great-grandparents are still alive would do well to persuade them to make oral recordings of their childhood memories and impressions. Otherwise, much of their family and cultural heritage will be lost. In this regard, ghost stories are treasure troves, thanks to the way they provide information about old houses, pre-pavement roads, family cemeteries, and so on.

For this book, I was able to collect ghost stories from individuals and from college and university archives in more than seventy counties across Kentucky, ranging from Ballard, Graves, and McCracken in western Kentucky, to Lewis, Greenup, Boyd, Lawrence, Martin, Pike, and Harlan in the Appalachian section. The bulk of stories in this book focus on ghostly events in Jefferson, Edmonson, Butler, Barren, Logan, Metcalfe, Monroe, Cumberland, and Wayne counties.

Ghost stories in this book focus on cemetery ghosts, return of family members as ghosts, benevolent ghosts, and other topics. These tales describe local life then and now, and the supernatural occurrences include dead persons returning as ghosts to seek vengeance, Civil War ghosts marching over gravesites, disappearing ghosts, and many others. Spelling errors have been corrected, but otherwise the accounts appear as told. Preceding each story is the name of the county where the events occurred; following is the name of the person telling the tale, as well as the town or community where the interview took place.

Over the years, southerners have relied on storytelling sessions as a means of entertainment. These told-to-be-true stories provide pleasure-filled events even to nonbelievers. So, sit back and read these stories, then tell some of your favorites during family and friendship get-togethers.

Notes

1. See William Lynwood Montell and students, *Mysterious Tales from the Barrens* (Glasgow, Ky.: JettPress, 1994), vi–vii.
2. Ibid., vi.
3. See William Lynwood Montell, *Ghosts across Kentucky* (Lexington: University Press of Kentucky, 2000), xvi.
4. Ibid., xvii.
5. William Lynwood Montell, *Ghosts along the Cumberland: Deathlore in the Kentucky Foothills* (Knoxville: University of Tennessee Press, 1975), 88–89.

1

Cemetery Ghosts

~

Dark Figure in a Cemetery

Hardin County

This is a true story that happened to me back in 2006. It's about the time some friends and I decided to go ghost hunting. We had heard of a place in Elizabethtown called Casey Cemetery, located on St. John Road.

It was a cool night when we got there. It's a creepy place at night, and it's old. No one has been buried there for years. We had some flashlights, a digital camera, and other things that might help us catch a ghost. Well, we had been there for about an hour when I and one of the others decided to go to the back of the cemetery.

One of the stories told about this place is that this spook will chase you if you go to the back end of the graveyard. So, we went and we sat around trying to hear or see anything unusual. Well, after awhile, we began to get bored, so we started back. The wind had gotten up, and I was trying to light my pipe, which kept getting blown out. So I turned back toward the back of the graveyard. As I was lighting my pipe, I caught a movement out of the corner of my eye, then said to my friend next to me, "I think I just saw a movement back there, so on the count of three let's put our flashlights on it."

So I counted to three, and we turned on our flashlights, and in the glow of the light we both saw what appeared to be a human figure with head, shoulders, part of a waist, but no legs. Yet it stood there for a moment, then began to move around a little. It moved only for the briefest of moments, then just disappeared.

We both saw that, and all we could do was stand there with our mouths open. Our other friends there saw nothing, but I would swear to God this truly happened to me and my friend.

David Allen Thomas, Glasgow, September 29, 2007

The Glowing Tombstone

Cumberland County

A long time ago, Lesley Phelps's Grandma Turner was walking down the road toward the bridge when she looked up and saw a tombstone glowing. She was so scared that she took off running. She was fine, but she saw that same tombstone glowing like that several times again.

After hearing the story one night, Lesley went to a slumber party and all of the girls there were walking down the same road in the dark. Lesley looked up and saw a tombstone that was glowing. It scared her so much the others were scared for the rest of the night. Lesley thought about her grandma's story and it scared her even more. That tombstone is still there, and if you go out walking down that road in the dark and look at that cemetery on the hill, you will probably see that tombstone glowing in the moonlight.

Kailey Phelps, Burkesville, November 1, 2007

Cemetery Ghost along Roadside

Cumberland County

One night these two men had been sitting up with a sick man in the community. After they decided to go home, one of the men had to walk home alone, and that was quite a distance. In the deep of the night something on the other side of the fence was walking right along beside him. He decided to run, but it ran along there beside him. When he stopped running, it also stopped running.

In trying to figure out who it was along there beside him, he assumed it was a dead man whose body was buried in a nearby cemetery.

Teresa Kirk, as told to Laura Kirk, Burkesville,
September 22, 2007

The Beheaded Ghost

Ballard County

My two brothers and I used to spend nights sitting around the lamp-light and listening to our father tell ghost stories. We lived about a half mile from our family burial ground named Bald Knob. There was no road to the cemetery, only a path made by dogs, rabbits, and perhaps a beheaded ghost.

Some nights the dead people came out of their graves to have parties. One dark and dreary night, not a star in the sky, the dead rose from their cold, soggy graves. It was not a happy night, and everyone was in a bad mood. Then the Big Man started a fight, as he often did. Before it was over, almost all of them were fighting, but the Big Man got the best of the others, and they finally got tired and crawled back into their graves.

For several weeks afterward, they did not come out again, but each one was thinking and thinking. When they came back out, they knew they were going to "get" Big Man, who liked to fight more than party. They waited and waited for the moon to be in just the right place. Finally, such a night came about. Even with the moon it was very, very dark, and the wind whistled around through the trees and tombstones. One by one they arose from their graves. They sat on their tombstones for a long time, no one saying a word. Finally, you could hear a small groan, a shrill shriek, a low moaning, and cries throughout the cemetery. It was so dark they could hardly see each other, but they knew where Big Man was! His grave was at the far side of the cemetery, and his marker was only a slab of concrete covering the gravesite. Huge pines stood near his grave, and an old owl was asking, "Who, who, who are you?"

A few animals were there and their eyes glowed in the darkness, but they scurried away upon hearing the owl and the restless dead. Fear was everywhere and who knew what was lurking nearby?

All at once, the dead people started walking toward Big Man as he came out of his grave, and the wind whistled and the rain started falling. Thunder and lightning kept Big Man from hearing them. Then all of a sudden, they jumped on him and tore off his head, then quickly ran back to their graves!

It is said that Big Man walks every night looking for his head. Even when the full moon is shining on his shoulders, he is there looking, looking, and the owl calls, "Who, who, where are you?"

At the end of the story, our father would offer us a nickel (one time a whole quarter) to go to the cemetery and bring back a pinecone from under the pine tree that stood near the Big Man's grave. We often considered it but never got farther than the steps of the back porch.

Our father put much emphasis and emotion in his storytelling, and the more scared we were, the better he liked it.

Mary Engler, as told by her father, Ed Kelley, January 29, 1992.
Courtesy of Folklife Archives at Kentucky Library,
John Morgan Collection, Western Kentucky University

Soldiers' Ghosts

Grayson County

I remember a couple of stories my dad told me. One of them is about the old cemetery in the Blotown community. Dr. Edmund Bryan is buried there. It is said that he is buried in a glass case, and there's a big slab over his grave. He died in 1863 during the Civil War.

Walter Cook, who is dead now, once owned the farm where the doctor's house once stood, and where the cemetery is located. Mr. Cook said he saw ghost soldiers marching over the grave at night.

Sandra Coates, Leitchfield, February 13, 1992

Storyteller's Personal Experience

Butler County

One winter morning I had to be at work in Morgantown by 6:00 A.M. I left home about 5:30. At the end of the road that I live on is Noah Johnson's cemetery. Right after I passed by the cemetery, I felt that someone was looking at the back of my head. The farther I went, the more I had this feeling of being watched. The feeling got so creepy that I finally stopped right in the road and turned the light on inside my car, expecting to see someone in the backseat, but no one was there. So I went on with that creepy feeling all the way to work.

Just as I came off the end of the Aberdeen Bridge on the Morgantown side, the back of my car seat pulled away from my back as though someone had pulled himself up by it to look out the window. I just sat there stiff and scared. As I passed by Jones Funeral Home, the seat just eased back up against my back as if someone had let go. I never knew what it was.

I think what happened was that I had given someone a ride to the funeral home. When I told my husband what happened, I don't think he believed me.

Judy Brooks, Morgantown, August 24, 2007

Was That Thing a Ghost?

Monroe County

I don't really know if this were a ghost, since I don't really believe in ghosts, but I do know this was an unexplainable occurrence. It has stuck with me since I was in my early teens and I have never forgotten how it looked, or what took place, so what happened is something that time has never erased.

This story took place on Halloween. We lived in Ebenezer and our house was really close to the Ebenezer Cemetery. When I was a teenager, a lot of times a group of my friends would meet at our house and just walk around the neighborhood and throw water balloons, put toilet paper on trees, and just have fun celebrating Halloween.

This specific Halloween, my sister Ramona and my cousin Mary and I were in our early teens, and we were to meet some of our neighborhood friends at my house. Since they had not got to my house yet, we decided to walk to the church cemetery and wait for them there.

Mary and I were walking side by side ahead of my sister, who was just tagging along behind us. There was a huge tree beside the Ebenezer Church of Christ and the cemetery. Just as we walked by the tree, a smoky transparent-like figure floated from behind the tree and just stopped in front of Mary and me. We both stopped and froze and started asking each other what is that, but my sister just kept walking and asking us what we were talking about. Mary and I started running and I was yelling for my sister to come on, that there was something in the road. She just kept walking and saying, "I don't see anything."

My cousin and I kept running, and I kept yelling for my sister to run, but instead she walked right up to where the transparent figure was standing. She stood there in front of the figure, then finally turned around and said, "I don't know why you all are running and screaming, because I don't see anything." She calmly walked back to our house.

When we got back to the house, our friends were on the porch and we told them about the incident, but they didn't believe us, and Ramona still to this day says she did not see anything either.

That is my little story and I have no idea what that was we saw, but it still stands out in my mind after all these years. They cut the tree down a few years later after this happened, so if the tree were the home where the spook lived, maybe it is gone, too.

Nedith Ford, Monroe County, August 31, 2007

Ghostly Lights

Monroe County

What I'm about to describe took place on election night several years ago. Of course, people used to drink whiskey a little back then. I hardly ever drank, but I did drink a little that night. And I wasn't easy to scare. That night, I drove back out to Mt. Gilead with Norman Miller. There was a path that cut through near the back of the church house. By taking the path, you could stay out of the road.

The path led up right close to the church house. When I got there, I saw a light in the back door of the church house. It seemed like while I was walking, I could hear somebody talking. I'd stop and look at the light, but couldn't hear a sound. Whatever it was didn't throw out light rays like a lamp, flashlight, or anything like that. It looked more like a ball of fire. I'd walk a piece and my nerves were sort of built up, so I wasn't a bit afraid.

Naturally, I didn't go up to it, but I went pretty close by where it was at. I'd walk a piece and hear something that sounded like somebody talking. I'd stop again, but couldn't hear a sound. But that light stayed right there.

I just went right on across the corner of the graveyard, a graveyard that didn't scare me much because I was used to it. I went to a one-room school right there by it. Since then, many a night I've walked right through the middle of that graveyard when I was going to Mt. Gilead to play pitch, rook, etc. While walking right through that graveyard, it never scared me one bit, and it didn't scare me that night, but I never did know what that light was all about, and still don't.

Willie Montell, Rock Bridge, 1974

Not a Real Ghost

Logan County

Not so long ago, this man was dying and he cursed his wife because she had made him so unhappy. Since the man didn't believe in divorce, he lived with her anyway. After he was buried, she never went to his grave. However, she kept hearing stories about the graveyard in which her husband was buried.

It was told that when they went to the man's grave, they were pulled into the grave and were never seen again. His wife didn't believe these stories, so she went out to his grave one night. She felt something grab her, and she had a fatal heart attack. When she was found the next day, they noticed that she had hung part of her clothing accidentally on a branch and apparently then thought she was being attacked by a ghost.

Jacque Tyler, as told to Judith Snow, Adairville, November 1954.
Courtesy of Folklife Archives at Kentucky Library,
Western Kentucky University

Ghost Returns to Grave

McCracken County

"Never whistle in the old cemetery" is the rule for folks that live around here. The reason for this is because of what happened one time. A man was walking through this old cemetery one dreary night on the way home from town. As he walked, he always whistled to help pass the time.

When he crossed the grave of a Negro still whistling, he heard a noise behind him. Standing there with his hands on his hips was a big old Negro ghost. The ghost said to him, "Can't I have no peace even while I'm dead? Now you stop that whistling noise or I'll find some way to do it for you."

With that, the ghost reentered his grave and left the man standing there with his mouth open. And after he told what had happened, no one who went to the cemetery ever whistled.

Richard Mills, as told to William Deaton, Paducah, 1972.
Courtesy of Folklife Archives at Kentucky Library,
Western Kentucky University

Preacher's Ghostlike Gravestone

Union County

About fifteen miles from Sturgis is an old church complete with grave-yard and squeaking planks inside the church proper. This haunted church also contains an old organ which was abandoned when the church moved to a more populous area of the county. The church is located along an old road that has not been traveled to any great extent in the past ten or twelve years.

It is rumored around the county that on a full moon one can go to the old church and hear the organ playing old church songs. These church songs were reportedly played by the last minister of the church, who was run off by the congregation just before the church moved. This is a very logical fact, because the minister was buried in the church cemetery after the church moved.

This place got to be such a harboring place for the youngsters around the area that a group of parents and county officials decided to tear the church down. The church was torn down, but they decided it would be unethical to destroy the cemetery also.

Now it is said that if one goes to the old cemetery on a full moon, the moon shines through the trees in such a way that only the gravestone of the minister, who was run off, shines in the moonlight. And for this reason, no one will again travel to the old cemetery at night.

Bill Lamb, as told to Bev Vance, Sturgis, 1970. Courtesy of Folklife Archives at Kentucky Library, Western Kentucky University

The Lone Grave

Bullitt County

There was a young girl that came from Mississippi to spend the summer months at Paraquet Springs, located on the banks of Salt River. While staying there, she met a young man with whom she deeply fell in love. During these hot summer months, the girl and boy would see each other every day. They would sit in a swing beneath the shade of the grove and share their love together. Soon the summer came to an end, and they returned to their homes.

They wrote each other as much as possible, and agreed upon a date to be married. The date was set for the following spring at the Paraquet Springs Hotel, where they would spend the summer together.

Shortly after their engagement, the young man became a soldier in the Mexican War, where he was killed in action. The girl grieved her loss bitterly and neglected her health. Finally, she knew that she did not have long to live, so she called her parents to her deathbed and asked them to bury her at Paraquet Springs under the beech tree, where she and her lover swang. She also asked them to put an iron fence around the grave, without a marker.

The lone grave remains there today under the shadow of the thick forest, with nothing remaining but the iron fence and the lone grave.

Ivy McBride, as told to Gary Reesor, Shepherdsville, ca. 1973.
Courtesy of Folklife Archives at Kentucky Library,
Western Kentucky University

Vincent Graveyard Ghost

Edmonson County

Me and Claudy Jaggers went out together, and we were riding mules. It was a real moonshiny night. We had been to a fellow's house located down in a big holler. When we come out of the holler, we come out right by the Vincent Graveyard, and there was big pine trees all growed up in the old graveyard.

Just as we rode out into the road, the mules got scared. We just looked across the road and seen something real white standing there by a tree. It looked like a man that looked to be seven or eight feet tall, and the thing was so bright it hurt our eyes. It moved around, [so we got away as quick as we could.]

I'll swear that's the truth.

Willard Jaggers, as told to Gary Watt, Chalybeate community, 1972.
Courtesy of Folklife Archives at Kentucky Library,
Western Kentucky University

Stone Angel's Activities

Hopkins County

There's an old cemetery in the Grapevine section between Madisonville and Earlington. The cemetery is on an old gravel road that isn't used much. Four of us drove by it one night, but nobody seemed to be anxious to stop. My sister and I and some other people went out there one day last year to look around, and went back again the same night. They found one grave that was opened, and it is supposed to be haunted by a blue light which follows people around after dark.

It is said that the occupant of the grave escaped and is now looking for somebody to take his place in that grave. He is supposed to pull or push anybody that comes near after dark to try to get them to tumble in.

In this same cemetery, there is a stone angel over a grave. This angel is supposed to move at dusk. She doesn't leave the scene, but she flaps her wings and moves her one remaining arm around. My friends and I have seen this. The night we went to see the angel, we tried to climb up on the stone, but an invisible force pushed us back down.

It is said that the angel guards a girl who was raped and murdered on a country road one night by three unidentified men. She won't rest until the names of those three fellows are known. The angel has only one arm now.

A few years ago, four boys from Madisonville went to this cemetery and managed to break or pull off the arm of the statue. The driver of the car in which they were riding had had his driver's license for only one day. They threw the angel's arm out of the car just before they turned onto Brown Road.

Moments later, their car overturned while in a high speed. Two of the boys died, and the other two were seriously injured. The two that died were the ones that did the damage to the statue. The other two boys had watched them do it, and helped in the getaway.

No one can prove that there is any relationship between the statue and the automobile accident, but it is something to think about. The ghosts of the two dead boys and the angel's arm are supposed to be visible on Brown Road on stormy nights.

Nancy Gray, as told to Jim Francis, Madisonville, 1972.
Courtesy of Folklife Archives at Kentucky Library,
Western Kentucky University

Child in the Cemetery

Mercer County

This ghost story was told to me by my Aunt Rosa Stephens. She has told it to her child and grandchild, her nieces and nephews, their children, and now their children's children. Her story never changes, nor is added to, nor taken from. Every time she tells it, she says she can see it like it happened yesterday.

Aunt Rosa's father was a minister, and was pastor of a church in Harrodsburg when Aunt Rosa was about ten years old. My Aunt Rosa and another little girl from the church had gone home with a little girl from Sunday School to spend the afternoon. They were walking back to church that evening, and it was dusky dark. They passed an old abandoned cemetery; the fence was broken down, and the cemetery was overgrown with weeds. You couldn't even see the graves. Everyone in Harrodsburg said it was an old black cemetery, possibly dating back as far as slave times. Aunt Rosa said they were right in front of the cemetery when a little black girl, who looked about three years old, walked over the broken fence in the cemetery and came on toward the girls.

Aunt Rosa has always been able to describe this little girl over the years, including the clothes she was wearing. She had on a little red jumper and a white blouse. Aunt Rosa said her first thought as the little girl kept walking toward them was why a little girl that small was out by herself at dark. As she got almost up to them, the little girl just disappeared. Of course, the girls were astonished and couldn't believe what they saw. Aunt Rosa said her dad had always told her to not get on the neighbor's grass, but she said that night the girls ran right through everyone's yard to get back to church.

The next day, Aunt Rosa told a young boy, who was a classmate, about seeing the little black girl. He challenged her to go back over there with him to show him where she had seen the little black girl, so he could prove there was nothing there.

When they arrived at the place where Aunt Rosa had seen the little girl, of course nothing was there. They climbed over the broken fence and went into the abandoned, overgrown cemetery. They saw nothing but old, old gravestones, until they were almost ready to leave, and over at the very back of the cemetery was a little grave, with a child-size headstone, but the name had long since worn off. That little grave was just the size for a three-year-old girl.

My aunt still tells this story just like she told it to me forty-five years ago, when I was about nine years old.

Connie Foster, told via e-mail, Russell County, January 31, 2008

Bray Cemetery Ghost

Monroe County

Right here close to where we are now is where Uriah Rasner lived. And he had a brother [Bill] that lived in what is called the Lee field. That is pretty close to what they call the Road House now, there on the Glasgow road. It's back this side a little.

And back in them days they didn't have any clocks, I don't think. Or everybody didn't have them at least. So, Bill Rasner, he's supposed to help his brother [Uriah] cut oats or wheat or something that day. That was back when they cradled their wheat. He got up and didn't have no clock, and he had to walk, so he thought he'd just come on. And he had a pack of hounds followed him. He got out here pretty close to this place we've been talking about tonight—Bray School House. And there is a little cemetery out there.

Back some time before that, [Bill] said he was going along there and something walked out in the road and it didn't have no head. And said them hounds kicked their tails between their legs and come running back to him and go behind him. He'd hiss at them but he couldn't get them to budge. And he said it didn't scare him much. He just kept walking and that thing just kept walking in the road out at a distance in front of him. And said that when he got on up this little graveyard there, why this thing just walked up in the graveyard and just disappeared.

He went on over to his brother's. And it was still dark. He'd started; didn't know what time it was. It wasn't near daylight and he laid down on the porch out there. Throwed some overcoats over him. Said them hounds was still scared to death. Said they just crept up all around him there. Well, anyway, he laid down there and went to sleep. And his brother waked him up after while, said the sun was shining.

He [Bill] told him that. And he [Uriah] wanted to know why in the world he didn't come in the house and go to bed.

He said, "Well, I just didn't want to bother you."

And they talked about that and he said they never could figure what it was, but it was a real ghost. And it was a ghost that the dogs could see and it scared them to death. Said they wasn't afraid of nothing. But they was scared that night!

Willie Montell, Rock Bridge, 1974

Gates of Hell

Hardin County

One night during this past summer, a group of my friends and I went down to Elizabethtown because we heard about a haunted graveyard there. The name of the graveyard is called Witches Graveyard, and is also known as Hells Gate. There is even a big stone with "Hells Gate" carved on it.

The history here goes back to the olden days, say around the time of the Salem witch trials, when E-town had its own share of trials. The so-called witches would be hung from a huge tree and then buried around it, which turned into the graveyard.

Some years later, murders took place there and there were horrible tortures. The place was eventually set to private property and soon forgotten about. But legend has it that when you go there at night and take a picture of the tree, when you develop your pictures, you will see people hanging. Also, it is said there are unexplained noises and sightings.

So this sounds like a great place to get your kicks, if you are into these kinds of things. So, of course, we go! It takes us about twenty minutes to get to it from the main road. You have to travel down a paved road, then a one-lane road, and finally a gravel road that ends at the gravesite. There is no way you would find this place by accident; someone would have to know about it in order to get there.

It's pitch black. We had no flashlights, just the lights by our cell phones. As we cautiously walked through it, we stumbled over aged tombstones until we came to the tree. The tree also reminded me of the tree of life from the Lion King. It had the biggest limbs I have ever seen. We took pictures and explored until we heard something that sounded like something fell from the tree hard. After that, we all booked it to our cars and got out of there as fast as we could. My heart didn't stop racing until we got on the main road again.

Every time I tell this story, I swear I will never go back. And as for the pictures, let's just say the legend is true.

Jaclyn Ray, Jefferson Community and Technical College,
Louisville, February 2008

Gates of Hell, Another Version

Hardin County

Near Elizabethtown, the cemetery at the end of St. John's Road is known as Gates of Hell, and is said to be haunted. The interesting thing about this haunted place is that when you travel to the cemetery, one of the last buildings you see is Elizabethtown's other haunted place, Bethlehem Academy. At the end of the road, which is no more than two miles, the road is surrounded by trees. This is where the overgrowth cemetery is located. It contains the graves of unknown people from the eighteenth and nineteenth centuries.

The place right outside the remains of the iron and stone gates is where people go to party away from town. Many years ago, while parked there at night, witnesses reported they watched an enormous green orb suddenly suspend right above them. After a couple of long minutes, the orb shot straight up so fast that it was out of sight in a second.

Others have claimed other phenomena while hanging out at the cemetery, such as screams, seeing shadowy people, and having electrical problems with their cars. It is said that many of the persons present when these things happen get so scared that many of them never return.

Ariel Cornette, Big Sandy Community and Technical College,
Prestonburg, February 2008

A Haunted Graveyard

Whitley County

My granny said when you disturb the dead, they will haunt you. I think that's true, because my whole family sees ghosts all the time. This story is about a graveyard on Cemetery Road in Williamsburg, Kentucky. My uncle Robert Taylor, my cousins Josh Parsons and Aaron Parsons, and their friend Walt Powers, decided to go to a haunted graveyard in 2002 on Halloween night. That's what our family does, so they did.

There was a big house right next to the graveyard, so they all decided to split up. Aaron and Josh went to the graveyard, and Robert and Walt went into the house.

As they entered the house, a gross smell was coming out of the rooms. They were walking through the rooms. When they came to this baby's room, in the crib was a baby crying. Walt walked over toward it and was going to pick it up and comfort it. When he got there, it was gone. Walt turned around and Robert said, "Dude, it's on you."

The baby had long nails and a gross face. Then the baby scratched Walt on the leg, and left a big mark on his leg, which he still has to this day. They went running out of the house, and Josh and Aaron were running out of the graveyard. They all ran to the car, then told each other what they saw.

Josh and Aaron told what they saw as soon as they got into the graveyard. They were walking around and saw a man smoking a cigarette, sitting on a headstone that had William Braham's name on it.

This fellow sitting there turned his head, and said, "What do you want? I'm trying to do this job for my family."

Then a woman appeared out of nowhere and said, "Supper's done; come and get fresh meat." Then the man stood up and started chasing the boys. They ran out of the graveyard back to the car.

Walt was hurt while running from the house, so they had to take him to the hospital for his wounds.

The story behind the graveyard is that a young couple back during the Civil War was living in this house when their newborn baby arrived. The husband was a grave digger. People that were running away from the war demanded to stay there in the house, but this young couple said no.

Well, one night, the young father was murdered on the grave of William Braham, and also his wife. These men then let the baby suffer and die.

Robert Taylor, as told to Lisa Tennison,
Corbin/Bowling Green, date unspecified

2

RETURN OF FAMILY MEMBERS
AS GHOSTS

~

Ghost of a Little Girl in a Tree

Barren County

This story was told to me by a very dear and close friend of mine, Junice Robertson. She said that when she was a little girl living here in Glasgow back around 1970—before everyone had air-conditioning—back then, families sat outside in the shade of a tree. She and her mother were sitting outside during a beautiful summer day. There was not a cloud in sight, but suddenly her attention was drawn to a large tree a few yards from them.

While she was watching, a little girl with blonde hair who was dressed in a white dress rose out of the trunk of this tree and ran to her mother and placed a flower in her lap. Junice had no explanation as to why she saw this. A few days later, while I was at her house, she mentioned this to her mother, who also said it happened.

David Allen Thomas, Glasgow, September 29, 2007

Grandfather's Ghost Smoked and Drank Coffee

Barren County

I have long heard that the old French restaurant, located on Harmony Hill, and also formerly called Patti's Restaurant, was haunted. The place was on Highway 90 toward Cave City, across from the airport near Glasgow. I often wondered why a restaurant would be haunted, so I asked the owners to let us spend a night there because of the rumors that it was haunted. They refused to let us do it. Being a curious sort of person, I was told this story by my dearest friend, Junice Robertson, and I believe her version. Junice told the story as follows:

"As a little girl, I remember my grandparents' house, located on Harmony Hill, and my grandfather was very proud of it and loved it a lot. It was my grandparents' very first home. My grandfather was a farmer, and I remember them going to barn dances and to general stores in and around Glasgow and Hiseville. As the years went by, Grandfather finally died, and the old home place became a business and restaurant.

"Grandfather always wore a dressy cowboy hat and long-sleeve button-up shirts, and he always chewed Moore's Red Leaf Tobacco. He also kept a cup of coffee with him, and I remember this well.

"It seems that after the house became a restaurant, workers there began having odd things that took place. For example, things they put here and there would be moved to other places, and when some of them were cleaning up at closing time, they would see this old man sitting at one of the tables with a cup of coffee, or chewing tobacco with a spittoon close by. On approaching the table, the workers saw no one sitting there. All they saw was someone vanishing into thin air.

"On one occasion, a worker was leaving work and got into his car and headed home. He saw my grandfather sitting in the backseat, and he then recognized him as the old man who always sat at the table. As he looked at the specter of my grandfather, he disappeared.

"I showed him a picture of my grandfather not long after that, and he turned white as a sheet, saying, 'That's the man we kept seeing.'

"The business is closed now, but one can't keep from wondering if the old man still sits there drinking coffee and chewing tobacco."

Junice Robertson, as told to David Allen Thomas,
Glasgow, October 1, 2007

Searching for Tooth

Wayne County

A long time ago, the Bell family lived on this farm, but they all died out. Years later, another family bought the farm. One day they were out plowing, and accidentally plowed up the grave of the mother of the Bell family.

They took the skull to the house and set it on the mantel. It wasn't long until a tooth fell out of the skull. During the following weeks there were many disturbances in the house. They were made by the ghost of the Bell mother, who didn't like the daughter in the family, and she pulled her hair.

That family finally had to move away because the ghost caused so much trouble when looking for her tooth.

Donita Crawford, as told to Bob Blanton, Monticello, November 18, 1970. Courtesy of Folklife Archives at Kentucky Library, Western Kentucky University

Loving Grandmother Returns

Ohio County

My senior year psychology teacher told me this. She and her sister shared a room that had two closets. One of the closets was theirs; the other was their grandma's, who lived with them until she passed away.

Their grandmother died when my teacher was seventeen years old, and her sister was nineteen. The night after the funeral, they were in bed, and my teacher woke up and saw their grandma walk across the room to her closet and take her blue sweater, the one she always wore when she was alive.

My teacher woke her sister up and they both saw their grandmother leaving. As their grandmother left, she looked back at them and said, "I love you and would never hurt you."

My teacher thought she had dreamed it, but after talking to her sister, she realized it had really happened. Then they went to their grandmother's closet and her blue sweater was gone.

Their mother told them that they should not be afraid, because their grandmother did love them and would never hurt them.

Jana Wilson, Centertown, March 22, 1989. Courtesy of Folklife Archives at Kentucky Library, Western Kentucky University

Aunt's Ghost Saves Nephew

Jefferson County

Steve, my boyfriend, had an aunt, his mother's sister. She was in a car wreck when, I think, she was in her early twenties. She was coming back home from Panama City for Christmas when she had the car wreck and died as a result. She was on the interstate coming back to her mother's house, and was only about forty-five miles from home. She fell asleep at the wheel and crossed over the median line, then had a head-on collision with a truck.

Steve and his grandmother spent the night there a couple of years ago. He got up to go to the bathroom and was walking down the hall. As soon as he passed his aunt's old room, he felt what was like a cloth; it swept his shoulder and went on past. He just stood there because he was so scared, and that was his first encounter with her ghost.

Well, he drove me down here on August 19, because I was a freshman and I had to be down here and all that rot. He left the next night at midnight, and was going to drive all the way back home, which is eleven hours away and he was just outside Nashville and was real sleepy. He was sleepy because he had left at midnight and he hadn't been to sleep at all that night. Because of that, he kept swerving off the road. One time when he was swerving off the road, he almost hit a sign. He had to get back on the road real fast.

The next thing he remembered, he found himself parked on the side of the road. He had obviously awakened but didn't remember pulling over. It was pretty cold inside his car, but it was pretty warm outside for August. When he got back to his senses, he looked down to start the car, but the keys weren't there. He looked all over the car for them and finally found them down underneath the seat. However, the ignition key that started the car wasn't on the keychain. So he looked up at the ignition and the key was in there, but it wasn't there before when he had looked.

Then he looked for his alarm clock that he always put on the dash, but it wasn't there. He wanted to see what time it was. He finally found the clock in the backseat, and the glass on it was broken. But if it had just fallen, likely the glass wouldn't be broken. So he looked at it and the time was 12:30, which was the time his aunt had died.

He started the car and it got warm inside again, and he began thinking that his aunt had something to do with him pulling off the road since he didn't remember doing it.

His mother and his grandmother claim that they, too, have seen her, or felt her presence.

Jan Humphrey, as told to Leslie Calk, Louisville, December 1970. Courtesy of Folklife Archives at Kentucky Library, Western Kentucky University

Images in Window

Logan County

In a huge castlelike house there once lived three sisters that were mentally disturbed, and their brother, who was a physician. The eldest of the three sisters was critically ill and was being treated by her brother for this illness. However, the brother was secretly poisoning her with the pills he was giving her. He gave them so slowly that when she died no poison would show up in the autopsy.

This sick sister called her brother to her bedside to read to her. While he was there, she died. Immediately, the shadowed image of the dead sister appeared on the wall of the sitting room. Upon seeing the image, the two other sisters went to their brother's study and found the pills that he had used to poison their sister. When the tea hour arrived, the sisters put all of the pills in their brother's cup. The brother drank the liquid and then died.

Immediately his shadow figure joined the shadow of the dead sister on the wall in the sitting room in the form of his sister lying in bed and him reading to her. The youngest sisters then commented on how it was so nice to have brother read to all of them again.

Jacque Tyler, as told to Judith Snow, Adairville, November 1954.
Courtesy of Folklife Archives at Kentucky Library,
Western Kentucky University

Return of Deceased Husband

Montgomery County

This story comes from a twelve-year-old boy. He and his family were living in a trailer park in Mt. Sterling. He was playing outside when his aunt called him in to eat dinner. His aunt's husband had been dead for two years.

After they finished eating and cleaning up the dishes, they were sitting in the living room talking when a figure walked through the door into the midst of the living room. The aunt immediately recognized the black-clad figure as her husband. He said he would take care of his widow for the rest of her life.

The young boy saw the figure again that night at the time he went to bed, but it did not speak to him.

Jeff Mitschele, as told by Tony Younger, Mt. Sterling,
November 28, 1970. Courtesy of Folklife Archives at Kentucky Library,
Western Kentucky University

Ghosts of Church Members

Graves County

Near Mayfield there's two churches built side by side, and they look exactly alike. However, one is older than the other. Back a long time ago, this family was on their way to church when they were all killed. The next Sunday morning they showed up in church as usual, and sat in the same pew.

People in the church got real scared and decided to close up the church and build a new one. They did, and today sometimes you can see the ghosts going to the old church on Sunday, while the church members are in the new one.

Dana Elliott, as told to William Deaton, Mayfield, 1972. Courtesy of
Folklife Archives at Kentucky Library, Western Kentucky University

Brother's Ghost Rescues Sisters

McCracken County

One time there was a fire at an old farmhouse, and one of the older boys was burned to death. They rebuilt the house and lived there for years with no particular problems. Then, one night, the house again caught on fire. Two of the girls were trapped in the upstairs area with no way of escaping, or anyone getting through to them.

Suddenly they felt a gentle arm reaching around each of their waists, and were carried out of the burning house. The ghostly being set them down on the ground beside the rest of the family. As the ghost flew away, it turned and waved and they saw it was the son that had been burned to death years before, when the first house burned.

Richard Mills, as told to William Deaton, Paducah, 1972. Courtesy of
Folklife Archives at Kentucky Library, Western Kentucky University

Ghost of the Well

Barren County

There was this man and woman who lived together for approximately seven years. They had a daughter whom the mother treated extra nice, and never did anything out of the way to hurt her. The wife/mother died, then the man remarried a few years later.

His second wife treated the child very badly, and would do anything mean and bad to her. One day, her stepmother was fixing supper when the little girl came in and asked her stepmother for a slice of potato. The stepmother slapped the girl across the mouth with the back of her hand, causing some bleeding, and the girl started crying.

When the stepmother went into the living room to finish her housecleaning chores, the girl was still crying. She could hear that the girl had stopped crying. The stepmother looked into the kitchen and saw a woman sitting in a chair, and the little girl was in her lap, being comforted by this woman. The woman was wiping the blood from the child's mouth, and she had on a white dress. When the woman who was taking care of the little girl noticed the stepmother, she disappeared, and the child was happy once again.

The woman told her husband what had happened, and the husband then told her that his first wife had said that if anything ever happened to their child, she would come back. Then, the man and his little girl went to the graveyard and opened up the coffin that her mother was buried in, and found blood stains on the white dress in which her mother had been buried.

After that, the stepmother never did anything wrong to the little girl again.

Bobby Runyon, as told to Mike Brannik, Glasgow, May 1972.
Courtesy of Folklife Archives at Kentucky Library,
Western Kentucky University

Mother's Ghost Remained at Home

McCracken County

Beverly's father, aunts, and uncles all used to live in a big house in Paducah. They lived with their grandmother, who moved in after their mother had died in the house. Their grandmother took care of them, just as their mother had. Three months after their mother had died, they started hearing a strange noise in the house. At first, they didn't think much about it, but later they decided that they all needed to get away from the memory of their mother.

They all left the house going their own ways, but grandmother decided to keep the house. Over a period of years, whenever any of the family went out into the country to visit the house, they would get an eerie feeling and hear strange noises.

Beverly's aunt decided to go to the house to get away from the city, and do her artistic paintings. She set up her easel in the living room and began painting. Then she started getting a funny feeling, being alone. She decided to move her stuff out into the front yard. Once she had done this, she took off her shoes and laid them next to her, then started painting. She began to hear faint screams coming from the house, and they grew louder and louder. She was so frightened that she left everything there and took off in her car.

During the next week it rained and rained. Streets were flooded, so the wind and rain caused people to stay home all week. After that, the first day it didn't rain, although puddles and mud were everywhere, she decided to return to the house to get her easel and shoes. She was still scared of the house, so she took her husband with her.

Once they got there, her easel had been blown down, and all of her paints and canvas ruined. She reached down to pick up her shoes, then screamed. Her husband asked what was wrong. Looking down, he saw that her shoes were perfectly dry, and looked as if they had never been wet, although there were puddles of water all around.

Beverly's aunt would never wear the shoes again, much less go near the house she believed was haunted by her own mother.

Molly Tuttle, as told by Beverly Haworth, Frankfort, April 5, 1973.
Courtesy of Folklife Archives at Kentucky Library,
Western Kentucky University

Death of a Man's Wife

Barren County

There was this man and woman who had just gotten married and had moved into this house that had an eighty-foot-deep well in the backyard. The man killed his wife and threw her into the well, then went to town to establish an alibi. The court decided that it was suicide and let him go.

When he went home later that night he heard a howl and a scream, then went out to investigate what was going on. He saw the figure of a woman jump into the well.

Later that year he remarried, and one night his new wife heard the same noises and saw the same figure, but the figure didn't jump into the well. It grabbed her and threw her in.

You can now see two women sitting on the well, almost every night.

Bobby Runyon, as told to Mike Brannik, Glasgow, May 1972.
Courtesy of Folklife Archives at Kentucky Library,
Western Kentucky University

The Dissatisfied Spirit

Morgan County

In a remote section of Morgan County, deep in a woodland area stands a crumbling old log cabin that once belonged to Uncle Davie. The land he owned was rich in timber and coal, so he decided he should make a will telling exactly how he wanted things divided when he died. This he did, and to protect and store this will and all his valuable papers, in the last years of his life, he built a large wooden box about six feet long and three feet wide. It looked like nothing so much as it looked like a handmade coffin, except that it was locked with a padlock, fastened with staples, deep into the wood.

After Uncle Davie died, the large box was moved to the loft of the old log house, still unopened because no one cared what Uncle Davie's wishes were now that he's gone. The grandson, Elisha, being the most aggressive of the descendants of Uncle Davie, just took over that old place. When he married, he brought his bride to the old log house to make it their home.

Uncle Davie, being a good old soul, wished his family to share alike, and not for one to hog it all. Elisha knew this, but he wasn't going to care now that Uncle Davie was dead and gone.

Elisha's wife liked the workmanship of the old box, even if it was still locked and no one cared to open it. So, some years later she had it brought down. She made a seat out of it, thinking she might as well get some use out of the old thing. It seemed as though the old box was settled for good the day Elisha's wife made a seat out of it.

Then it was twelve o'clock noon. Things were quiet after the meal, everybody enjoying their rest before going back to work. There were Elisha, his wife, their son (who was a strapping boy twelve years old), and a friend of the family all sitting around talking quietly. At the exact stroke of twelve on the old wall clock, the chest suddenly raised itself clear off the floor about six inches and came down with a thud to stay quiet again.

Elisha's wife, being sort of sensible, thought the boys were pranking with them as they seemed to be closest, so she scolded them. They all said they didn't do anything. Elisha suddenly turned white as a ghost, muttering something about Grandpa and his ghost. Of course, nobody believed him.

The next day at exactly twelve o'clock, the old clock struck and the box again raised itself up six inches in the air. Always, at the exact stroke of twelve every day, the old box raised up. The family was getting scared to death, and no one would go near the old box.

One day the boys decided they would try to keep the box on the floor, so they both got on top and stretched out five minutes before twelve, thinking their weight would hold it on the floor. They waited, scared almost to death.

At exactly twelve when the clock made the stroke, the box raised up six inches off the floor, boys and all, then was quiet again. Several people had come in to see the haunted box, and saw the box jump up. Instead of being afraid now, the family seemed to enjoy the fame of Grandpa's ghost in the old box.

The family lived there 'til they were old, but no one, no matter how brave, dared to open the box to let out Grandpa's ghost, as it continued to bounce exactly at twelve. Elisha, however, would never go near the old box, and Grandpa's ghost seemed to plague him more and more as the years wore on.

One night when his wife was dying, a neighbor and his wife were sitting up with her. The lamplight was dim and the fire was down to just a bed of red coals. A large bucket of coal was sitting on the hearth; wood was piled high on top of the coal. The neighbors sat silently, staring in the fire. Suddenly, the bucket, wood, coal, and all went up in the air about six inches and came down again with nary a stick of wood out of place! Elisha's wife was dead.

With the passing of his wife, Elisha housed himself with the ghost of Grandpa 'til he died in the old house that was crumbling to decay. But strange enough, the old box still leaped up on the stroke of twelve to tell people that there was still a dissatisfied spirit roaming in the old home atmosphere.

Virginia Cox, as told to Helen Elva Mink, location unspecified, 1960.
Leonard Roberts Collection, Southern Appalachian Archives,
Berea College

Treasure Never Found

Henderson County

Some folks believe that Charles Winfrey's ghost still stands guard over the bags of gold that he supposedly hid on his farm, located between Owensboro and Henderson on the eastern side of the Green River.

Winfrey, a wealthy bachelor who set no store in paper money, was murdered in September 1864. He was taken to a house on the back part of his farm and shot. Although he lived about an hour after he was found, he was unable to say who his assailant was. His gold was never found.

Mr. Winfrey owned five farms, two so-called tobacco factories, eighteen to twenty-five slaves, and had income of $15,000 a year. It was common knowledge that he did not trust paper money, nor banks, and transacted business only with hard money, which he kept somewhere on his property.

In an attempt to gain their legal share of the money that Winfrey was thought to have accumulated through hard business deals, his heirs filed suit. There are on file at the Henderson County Courthouse more than a hundred pages of claims and counterclaims concerning the case.

Many believed the gold was still on the property. A slave told that Winfrey had blindfolded him and made him dig a hole in the ground and bury bags of money. As a result of this slave story, digging continued on this farm for seventy-two years. Somebody even dug up Winfrey's vault. Pieces of it are still in the farmyard today.

People who did the digging reported numerous instances of seeing a ghostlike image of Winfrey. Winfrey's neighbors, Lewis and Uni Remole, who lived directly across the road, sought diligently to recover the lost property for themselves. It is said they went so far as to invoke the aid of the spirits in their search. They would pray, asking the spirits to tell them where the money was hidden, then they would proceed to dig.

Apparently they never found any money, but as they grew older they began to fear that someone, or something, was trying to kill them. To protect themselves, they hired a bodyguard to stay with them until they died peacefully.

Ralph Dorris, as told to Jim L. Clark, Owensboro, February 7, 1969.
Courtesy of Folklife Archives at Kentucky Library,
Western Kentucky University

Foot Tickling Ghost

Kenton County

This took place in the Covington/Newport area. What I'm about to describe happened to my sister-in-law and her sisters many times. She and her sisters used to room together in a home that used to house her recently deceased grandmother. The door would creep open, and Shelly, my sister-in-law, would cringe when a cold feeling would sweep over her. She would hold steady to the covers, but her feet would be slightly exposed. A few moments later she would feel something grasp her foot. Struggling would never release her from this fate. Suddenly a cold hand would begin tickling her exposed feet. She would do all she could to stop from giggling, but for some reason that never worked.

Each time she began to laugh uncontrollably, a white face would creep up from the end of the bed. The face would be clear and white, but it had a sad expression. Then, all of a sudden, the figure would smile, pat the foot, then dismiss itself. That figure was very much her grandmother.

Today, my sister-in-law is afraid to sleep with her feet hanging over the bed.

Source and date unknown

3

Haunted Houses and Public Buildings

~

Roadhouse Ghost

Barren County

Roadhouses were common back in the early years of pioneer Kentucky, on up until the early 1900s. This is a story of one such place where a person could get a room for the night; something to eat and maybe drink, or just unwind after many days of traveling. Most people would stay one night there, maybe two. However, in this story, as told to me by Junice Robertson, who lived in this house, someone decided to make it a permanent residence long after death.

"In the winter of 1984–85, I moved into a house on the Glasgow–Park City Road. The people that owned the house told me they took so long to decide to rent it to me because it was haunted, and they wanted me to know before taking it. So I took it.

"Not long after moving into it, I noticed that when I laid things down they would be moved around. I had a table where I would put on makeup. If I put my mirror on the table and left the house, sure enough, when I came back my mirror would be on the stove. This happened many times.

"I used to wear contact lenses, and every night I went to clean them after turning on my lamp, and waiting a couple of hours for the machine to clean them. Before bedtime I would find that the lamp I had turned on would be off.

"On another occasion, my young son and I went to a neighbor's house to use her phone since I didn't have one. I put one of his shoes on him, and looking high and low I could not find the other shoe anywhere. After using my neighbor's phone and visiting, I went back home and unlocked the glass door, but it would not open. I thought there was something wrong with the doorjamb, but then the door opened inward, not out. After pushing it awhile, I noticed the door was moving away from the jamb, but something seemed to be stuck in the middle of it. So I pressed my face up against the glass of the door and looked inside. Behold, there was my son's other shoe up against the door on the inside of the house.

"Things like that went on all the times I lived there, but after awhile it became clear that whatever it was meant me no harm. On one occasion, I had someone that tried to scare me, then left and came back that night. My friendly ghost scared them so bad that I was told by them they would not sleep with the lights off after that night.

"After that, I no longer feared the spirit that made this place its home."

Junice Robertson, as told to David Allen Thomas,
Glasgow, October 1, 2007

Ghostly Visitation

Four other men and I went to work in a new location. We rented a room in a boarding house, but soon found out it was rumored that the house was haunted because a woman was killed there. The owner told one of the men with me that he might hear some strange noises. The man said, "I'll take care of it."

That night the same fellow was sitting on the couch reading the newspaper when he heard the door open and heard footsteps, but didn't see anything. Then, the coffee table started shaking and something grabbed the newspaper from his hands, wadded it up, and threw it into his lap. He grabbed his shoes and immediately left with a shoe in each hand.

Jesse M. Mings, as told to Beulah Cox Mings,
location unspecified, date unspecified

Battletown Elementary School Ghost

Meade County

We live in a small Meade County community called Battletown, and legend has it that there is a ghost in our school. We have learned in our research that the ghost used to work here, and loved the school. Now she comes back to visit. Here are some stories we heard.

This one is from our kindergarten and first-grade teacher, Mrs. Halen. She was here by herself one night after the sun had set and said she heard chimes ringing down the hallway in one of the classrooms. She went to see if anyone was there, but nobody was there, and the chimes were just moving by themselves.

Another story we have heard is from one of our lunch ladies, Mrs. Sipes, who has worked here for thirteen years. She said, "Years ago, we had a screen door that wasn't locked and it would just open and close by itself." They said they knew it was the ghost, so they just said, "Hi," and went on with their business. Now we have a big door that we keep locked, so the ghost has to knock before she comes in, and when they open the door there is no one there, so they just let her in and keep on cooking.

Another story that we have about the ghost in the kitchen is that we had a frying pan setting on the stove, and it just picked up and set back down again.

The next story we have about the ghost is that the lunch ladies have a Christmas tree decoration setting on top of our freezer in the kitchen and when someone walks in front of it, it sings Christmas carols. The lunch ladies were in back of the kitchen and no one was in front of the Christmas tree when it started playing Christmas carols.

We have a story from one of our substitute teachers, Mrs. Sith. We have three windows with blinds over them in our computer lab, and she was in our computer lab by herself one day and said that the middle blind came out and SLAMMED back against the window. The window wasn't open and the air conditioner wasn't on!

Another ghost story that we have is about Anna-lee, Kim, and some friends. All of them were riding in the van from church one night. They were going to drop a friend off that lived past the school. When they passed the school they thought they saw something. When they came back through, they saw the kitchen light on. No one was there, and no one left it on.

Here's a story—our class voted on to put in this story. One time, one of our classmates was in the bathroom by herself and she said that all of the stall doors opened and closed at the same time by themselves.

There are many stories, but let us tell one that we think is really weird. A teacher in our school named Mrs. Lancia once said while she was in the school after hours, she had her dog with her. Suddenly her dog started to growl and bark, and its hair was standing straight up. She looked out the door and saw nothing at all outside of her door. The weird thing is that her room is beside the cafeteria, where the ghost is seen and heard the most.

There are many other stories about the ghost of Battletown Elementary School, but we think these are the most interesting.

Ashlyn Mills, Hannah Skaggs, and Kyla Arnold,
Battletown, October 2006

The Haunted Fireplace

Butler County

When my mom was a child, her parents moved the family into a house here in Butler County, a house that had not been lived in for awhile. They moved there in the early summer. The house had four rooms, which was a large sized house back then. It also had what they called back-to-back fireplaces in it. One was on the kitchen side; the other was on the living room side, and they both used the same chimney. Grandma used the one in the kitchen for cooking, but because the weather was warm, no fire had been built in the other one.

When the weather started getting cooler, my grandfather built a fire in the living room about dark one night. As soon as the fire got to going real good, everyone heard a baby crying. My grandmother thought at first that someone had left a baby outside the door, but when she looked she could not find anything. Then they noticed that the closer you came to the fireplace, the louder they could hear the baby crying. She made my grandfather put the fire out, and the crying actually stopped.

The next night was the same way when he built the fire. Then he took all the brick out of the front of the fireplace and replaced them with some others. Still, when a fire was started, so did the crying. Because of that, Grandmother refused to have a fire in the fireplace during the rest of the winter.

They spent a very chilly winter, and moved out in the early spring. Later they found out that the last family that lived there had a small child about two years old that fell into the fireplace and burned to death before her parents could get her out.

Judy Brooks, as told by her mother, Morgantown, August 24, 2007

Ghost of a Baby Boy

Ballard County

Grandmother always told about the time she and Grandfather were coming home one night from somewhere. They were in a horse-drawn wagon. They went over this bridge while it was raining and was really foggy. They drove by this house where a baby had died a couple of months ago. Back then, all the houses had porches on them.

As they passed by, they saw this baby out on one of the porch columns. It was running around, kind of swinging around the pole. The baby they saw was a little boy, but it had on a dress. Back then, boys wore dresses as well as little girls until they got to a certain age.

I can remember Grandma telling me about seeing the baby boy. It was just as clear as anything that she and Grandfather both saw it. That little baby that had died was swinging around the support column of the porch.

Patsy Terrell, as told to Linda K. Adams, Ballard County,
July 22, 1990. Courtesy of Folklife Archives at Kentucky Library,
John Morgan Collection, Western Kentucky University

The Joe Russell House

Metcalfe County

We had just moved into this house, and we were all very tired. So we went to bed, and something came to the front door and liked to have torn it down. Whatever it was then went to the back door and liked to have torn it down. We had a full-sized basement, and we cooked down there also. We thought we left our dog, Tina, down there in the basement. We heard something throwing our pots and pans from the stove to the table, and then to the cabinet.

Every time it rained, a light came across our big window in the living room. It was as big as the glass in the TV set. We also began to hear something like cows in the barn. We would go to the barn the next morning and there would be everything just like it was. Dad said it was nothing. So, once he slept all day, and said he would stay awake all night. And he did.

My grandma, Mama, me, Elvin, Teresa, and Dad were all in the same bed when morning came. Dad had slept with a knife in his hand all night. We had lived there for only two months, and Dad said we would be moving in about two weeks.

Some other people lived there after that, but for only two months. They heard the same thing we did. They are good friends of ours. We said that two months is the limit, and so did they. No one is living there now.

Kathy Glass, as told to Kay Harbison, Summer Shade, 1969

Mysterious Door Latch

Monroe County

My sister stayed at a place in which the doors had these old wooden drop latches. She was told that the door to her bedroom would come open by itself. Well, she didn't believe that. But after she moved in there, each night when she'd go to bed that latch would raise up and the door would come open. There was nobody there. It was those old wooden latches on the door.

When she'd go to bed, she knew there was nobody there in that room but her. She'd hear the latch make a sound, then the door would open. She said that was true; that latch would raise, and she could hear the door come open.

Darlene Carter, Rock Bridge, 1964

Strange Doors and Windows

Hart County

My uncle had a place where he lived, and it was way back in a bend in the Green River. There was only one way by land to get to it and that road traveled up a big hill and down to a flat area that was surrounded by the river. That was where the house was located. The house looked very common, but in truth was far from it.

Very strange and unexplained events occurred every night. The door and windows could not be kept shut by any means at all. Locked, bolted, and even driving 10-penny nails in the window sills were unsuccessful. Each would be wide open and the nails lay in the floor as if pulled right out of the cardboard.

Everyone that slept there would be awakened during cold evenings, not only by the open door and windows, but something or someone would pull all the bed covers off the bed. My aunt had slept almost all night, then was awakened as the quilts were being pulled off of her. She was convinced she could stop this, so she grabbed for the covers, but didn't get them at all. She grabbed what she said was the coldest and clammiest hand she had ever touched in her life.

For as long as I knew her, she never forgot that, and never spent the night there again. Those events occurred for years, but somehow the house caught fire one evening and burned to the ground. Luckily, no one was at home when it burned.

Jeff Jaggers, as told by anonymous male, location unspecified, 1993

Ghostly Hospital Room

Floyd County

Workers in any hospital form a sort of community and society all their own, with social rules, mores, and even myths and legends such as ghost stories. A hospital is in fact the most logical setting for such tales, for what other building in the world regularly and consistently hosts so many deaths within its walls? In consideration of this, perhaps it is unusual that a community of workers in a single hospital create and collect relatively few ghost stories. However the ones that do manage to survive in a hospital's culture are generally doozies.

One of the most unsettling experiences I ever had personally at work was a chance circumstance in which two "code blues," that is, cardiac/respiratory arrests, occurred simultaneously on one of the most bitterly cold nights of a very inclement winter. During the labors of the two code teams, the lights flickered on and off, one elevator dropped to the basement and sat there, its doors opening and closing, opening and closing, and all of the freak phenomena could be attributed to the extreme cold weather. But still, who could tell? Even so, that story cannot compare with the tale of Room 424, a private room in a certain eastern Kentucky hospital.

After the building was remodeled in the 1960s, it seemed that the malignant entities in the place found other quarters. At least they began to be quiet. But for a few years, a sojourn in Room 424 was a brush against the shroud of evil.

It seemed that everybody that spent a night in Room 424 was made the worst for it. Sane, sensible people would go in as patients and come out shaken and disoriented in the morning, complaining of children dressed in white walking around the room's bed, faces peering in the outside windows, lights flickering off and on, and bizarre whispers. A lot of people died in that room, the most memorable of which was in the wee hours of one morning. It was the death of an old lady who lived in a county or two away, and for whom the undertaker from that county was delayed for two or three hours.

Hospital policy dictated that an aide would stay with the body until the undertaker arrived. However, the service was shorthanded that night, so the charge nurse respectfully laid the body out on its back, tucked sheets and blankets over it, pulled the bed curtain all the way around the bed, turned out all the lights and closed the door, leaving the room and the body alone for more than an hour.

When the undertaker finally arrived on the floor, the charge nurse sent them to the room, but they immediately came back to the nurse's station claiming they couldn't get the door open. Concerned and thinking that perhaps a visitor had somehow evaded everyone's eyes and blundered in there, the charge nurse, whom I personally know and worked with for several years, went to the door and tried to force it open. Although the door opened, she later claimed that it felt almost as if someone was on the other side pushing. And when she and the undertakers entered, to her horror she found that something or someone had turned on the bathroom light, with the fluorescent tube flickering as if it had a bad electrical connection; the covers had been pulled off the body; the body itself was lying not on its back as she had left it, but on its face.

It would have taken a sick, sick vandal to rearrange the room in that fashion, and that is the logical explanation for the tale, in fact the only logical explanation. But again, who really knows?

John Sparks, location unspecified, December 11, 2007

The Crying Baby

Grayson County

My grandmother, Minnie Henderson, was really a master at storytelling, especially ghost stories. She told several, but the one she related often, and I remember clearly, is about a haunted house she and her husband and family lived in. This house was located in the small town of Caneyville in Grayson County, and would have likely been in the 1920s. My grandmother said they had moved to Grayson County, I believe because of work that my grandfather was doing, and rented a house that was located across the railroad track in Caneyville.

After moving in and getting ready for bed that night, they heard what they thought was a child crying. After checking their own children and seeing it was not them making the crying sound, they started looking. It almost sounded as if it was coming from outside the house. My grandfather went all around the house and could find nothing, but while he was outside, he noticed the sound seemed to come more from the inside! They could not find the source of the crying, but it went on night after night.

My grandmother told her father about what was happening at the house into which they had moved. He told her he thought someone was trying to scare them off from the house, and his guess was they had attached a resin string to the house somewhere and were using it to make the sound when they went to bed. He further said he would come and spend the night to see if it went on while he was there.

Sure enough, when the family went to bed, the crying started. My great-grandfather, feeling sure he could find the source, went outside. He took a long pole and went all around the house to see if anything was attached that could be used to make this noise. Nothing was found!

My grandmother concluded the story by saying as long as they lived there, this sound of a child crying continued, and they never discovered what, or who, it was.

Connie Embry, Roundhill community, December 16, 2007

The Old Home Place

Wayne County

At one time I owned the old home place where my great-grandfather settled when he came into this country. My mother and I were both born on this place. Then later, I lived about four miles from here, but I still planted my garden at the old home place. One day, I had decided to be brave and go work in the garden by myself. It came up a rain, so

I had to go inside the old house. I decided to do some cleaning while I was waiting for the rain to stop.

There was a closet next to the fireplace, and an old clock on the mantel which had not run for years. My father had told me every now and then the old clock would strike. The closet door was open when I went in, so I closed the door. It was always really dark in this closet, so I went about my cleaning.

Every time I went through that room, the closet door would open, so I closed it five or six times. Then I noticed something strange; every time the door came open, the old clock would strike. So I left before the rain stopped!

Some time after that, some friends were there with me. The closet door came open and the old clock started to run real fast for about twenty minutes, then stopped. That was very, very strange, so I brought the old clock home with me. It has been in the family for ninety years.

Oleva Morrow Catron, as told to Chris Cook, Coopersville, 1993

A Spooky House

Fayette County

This is a story about what took place when I was a little girl about ten years old. The street behind the house where we lived had an old house located on Tahoma Road in Lexington. There was a lady that had lived there, but she moved to Florida, supposedly because her little girl had gone outside to a little pond [in the yard]. It was kinda like a fishbowl, and the little girl drowned in it. But the story goes on to tell that something like a demon or something pulled her under.

The old house was real old and creepy, had vines growing up all around it, and the grass was always not mowed. We could look inside the letter box that was on the door. We could lift it up and look inside the house, and when you looked in there, we always saw a light on the right at the top of the steps. You could see the living room if you looked real hard in the daytime, and there was candy in dishes that were always on the table. The chair there by the table, and the table itself, always looked like they had just been cleaned.

The strange part about it was that nobody lived there then. It was always real musty smelling, and there was always a kind of a cold feeling there. I mean that was when I was little and stuff. It was spookier then than I guess it would be now. But that was when I was little and we used to walk there and scare ourselves to death.

Tory Combs, as told to Leslie Calk, Lexington, 1972.
Courtesy of Folklife Archives at Kentucky Library,
Western Kentucky University

Shaking Stairway

Butler County

This was supposed to have taken place on a farm near Morgantown. It was said that no one could ever live in this old doctor's house, because he was killed by the hands of someone unknown. His throat was cut while sitting in a rocking chair in his office.

My uncle and a man by the name of Tom Pitcock were both bachelors and had leased the farm and moved in the next day. It was raining that day and Tom had gone to town, so my uncle decided he would go into the doctor's office and get a book to read. He said when he picked up the book something seemed to fall over him, as though he had been hit. The stairs began to shake so hard that they made the whole house shake. My uncle dropped the book right there. He said there were lots of books in the room, and the rocking chair still had blood on the back of it.

The following day, Tom left again and it was still raining, as like the day before. Night came on and Tom hadn't returned home. Then my uncle heard someone whistling coming up to the house. He said in front of the door it sounded like someone threw a wood pole down. He waited awhile, thinking it was Tom, then he went to the door and said, "Tom, you can't scare me, so you might as well come on in."

Daylight came, and still no Tom. Along up in the day Tom came, and my uncle told him what happened and that he could have his part of the lease, but Tom told him he didn't want it. So my uncle told him that he was leaving, and Tom said, "So am I."

Jacob Curtis, as told to Robert Curtis, 1970.
Courtesy of Folklife Archives at Kentucky Library,
Western Kentucky University

Woman in White

Adair County

My two youngest brothers were spending the night at our neighbor's house, where everybody thought it was haunted by the woman that used to live there before she died. They went in, and then this woman dressed in white walks in. She just stood there and looked them over; never said a word. She stayed there for about fifteen minutes, then turns around and walks away. My brothers didn't say anything to each other about it.

Finally, one of them was talking to our neighbor when he spoke up and said he had seen the same thing, too.

James Keltner, as told to Glenn E. Groebli, location unspecified, 1971.
Courtesy of Folklife Archives at Kentucky Library,
Western Kentucky University

Haunted by a Nun

Hardin County

There is an old building seven miles outside of Elizabethtown that used to be an all girls school taught by nuns. The name of the school was Bethel Academy and has been abandoned for fifty or sixty years. The place is very far from any houses and farms, so in the first years of the school the girls had to live there during the school period, so this gives information that this was quite a large structure. The building is three stories high with the assembly room on the top floor, and also an organ and other musical instruments.

When the school was closed and abandoned for good, three nuns stayed in their quarters until they could get another job. Then it was winter, and in that time of the century at night there was not a whole lot to do. Therefore every night one of the nuns would go to the assembly room to play the organ for enjoyment and practice.

One night while one of the girls was playing, the other two nuns heard a scream from the third floor. The blood curdling scream terrified the other two so badly they would not go to the assembly room for anything. They told themselves it would be wise to not go up there because there had been talk of a mad man on the loose.

The next day, they got the neighbors to come over and check the upstairs. When they reached the room, there lay the nun over the organ without her head, and lying in a pool of blood.

These days, the place is considered haunted by the nun. One thing that seems to be her ghost is that the trees in front of the academy have never had leaves on them since her death. Also, on a real windy and cloudy night, the ghost is supposed to be seen in the top window around the organ.

Penny Vance, as told to Bev Vance, Hodgenville, 1970.
Courtesy of Folklife Archives at Kentucky Library,
Western Kentucky University

Unknown Ghost

Daviess County

There was an old house outside of Owensboro owned by a very respectable family in the community. A few years back, the man decided to add on a new part to the old and tear down some of the old. After the expansion was done, the girl in the family still slept in the old part of the house.

One night she went to bed and everything was locked as usual. Later that night the family heard screams coming from that room, but it was locked on the inside and they could not enter nor get her to come to the door. After awhile there was silence. The father and mother were very scared for their daughter, but the next day the girl remembered nothing, and also her door was opened when she got up.

This was not the only incident that happened in that house. When the family moved furniture around in the old part of the house, then walked away, the furniture was always rearranged back the way it was to begin with.

Bev Vance, as told in psychology class at Western Kentucky University,
1970. Courtesy of Folklife Archives at Kentucky Library,
Western Kentucky University

Female Ghost Pretender

Henderson County

We heard that a ghost was frequenting a place where it had never been seen, but had acted. An old lady had died there recently, and she had always folded her clothing pieces nicely, and laid them over a chair. She then set her shoes side by side under the bed and laid down and died. So it was said, if you or anyone else moved a piece of her wearing apparel or shoes, something placed it right back where it was.

The house was on the old Raffity place just across the Laydanne Bridge, a little iron bridge over Panther Creek. Long ago it was a regular place, but it was old now and decaying, located near Rome or Panther, Kentucky.

My father rented the land and batched there one summer, leaving the old lady's bedroom securely locked, as all he wanted to do was cook a bite, and sometimes he and my brothers spent the night to get to work early. The boys peeped in at the window and declared they saw things.

It so happened that the place was covered with ripe blackberries, and an orchard of fine apples. So we (my mother, two boys, and my baby girl of three years) packed a lunch, put the children in a buggy, and took off for the old farm. Dad and the boys were at home in Owensboro, and we meant to stay only that day. Well, our buckets were soon full of delicious fruit, but it began to pour down rain, and we soon saw we would have to spend the night, regardless of the reputation of the house.

Mama was very uneasy about me and the children. She knew there was plenty of food for supper and breakfast, but she did not want any unnecessary scares one way or another. My boys were just at the age to be in a lark, so they brought the ax in just in case it was needed to help make the beds and care for us all. However, none of us intended to sleep a wink; we would sit up as long as we could for fear some unusual thing would happen.

We never went into that bedroom, nor had any inclination to go in. However, there were so many noises that one would scarcely know just what they were. An electrical storm made everything worse, and did it rain! When it lightened, you could see the creek rising, which made us wonder if it wasn't a flood.

What a predicament I was in! My mother was there, my three children, my horse and buggy, many gallons of fresh berries with no way to care for them, and no idea when the rain would ever let up. With no parasol, and ten miles from home, and a muddy road and a night to go through, weariness was setting in.

One after another of the little kids' heads drooped, and finally all were asleep but me. I was truly thankful, as I could manage anything better when alone. The clock pointed to eleven and the lights were out. Several men stomped and stomped as if they were getting rid of mud. This brave little me was all that was left to protect the sleepers, so I headed to the door in a long, white nightdress, hair streaming all over my shoulders. My face was white as death. As best I could make out, there was a yard full of men. I could only see them when it lightened, but they also saw me and they were far more frightened than I was, and they left there in a drenching downpour of rain.

Common sense began to assert itself, and I just imagined they were gamblers and had come to where they could gamble unmolested. The ghost I invented had been to frighten them away. But when they saw me, the ghost truly came alive to them, and they vacated. I slept as lightly as possible, praying all my waking hours.

It rained all the next day, and the creek rose and covered the yard. We ate potatoes and cornbread, and drank coffee. Our berries had soured. Our horses were well stabled and well fed. But no one would take them to drink water. When Dad drove in with provisions and more nice bed coverings, I knew no more. I went to sleep and Mama fixed a delicious meal. The news would keep until an appropriate time, which was not right then.

We spent another night; the rain had ceased and the creek went down, and a sadly bedraggled bunch of people went home. An investigation was made, and it proved out that shady deals had been going on there, but many of the dealers still believe they saw a ghost in white, and you could not get them near the old house again.

The house burned late that fall, and I wished I was able to buy that lovely old place for a home, even if it was almost submerged that night. The land was soon properly drained and the changes that have taken place have hurt the beautiful and picturesque for at least one artist, my daughter Sarah.

Sena Smithhart, as told to Jim L. Clark, Henderson, February 21, 1969. Courtesy of Folklife Archives at Kentucky Library, Western Kentucky University

Bothered, Bothered, and Then Some

Ohio County

Jerry had a farm in Ohio County on which stood a new house made of concrete blocks. Next door to it stood an old frame of a true cabin, which he knew nothing about its background. He told about how beautiful the land was. He heard no noises at night except those from crickets and frogs. He worked the farm himself during the daytime, and sometimes would spend the night in the cabin.

When you entered the third room of the house, you immediately feel a cold chill. Even if you stood half in and half out of the room, the part of your body in the third room would quickly become cold. Jerry felt that something was wrong with the house and did not like to stay alone in the house at night. The first night he stayed in it, he felt a strangeness come over him, and did not sleep well.

The second night Jerry spent there was one even more restless than the night before. He was awakened in the middle of the night by two friends that said they had received mental telepathy that he was in some kind of trouble; thus, they got dressed and rushed right over. When they got there, they found Jerry turning over and over in his bed, covered with perspiration. Not only had the third room been cold, but the whole house gave off a chill. The friends remained with him for the rest of the night. They all claimed that when morning came, the chill was gone in all rooms except in the third room.

The next day, Jerry made a cross of wood and took it into the house to see if whatever possessed the house would still remain in the house with the cross in it. He claims that the feeling left the house when the cross was brought in.

Even though Jerry believed the wooden cross helped, he never spent the night there again.

Molly Tuttle, as told by Jerry Keller, Bowling Green, April 3, 1973.
Courtesy of Folklife Archives at Kentucky Library,
Western Kentucky University

Young Lovers Killed

Logan County

One rainy night a traveler stopped at this large house hoping to spend the night to get out of the bad weather. The house was empty and badly in need of repair. While eating, he heard steps, then a beautiful young girl and a young man walked in. They were real upset and were talking softly. Then, she started crying, and the young man started kissing her and trying to comfort her. Suddenly, loud steps were heard and a huge middle-aged man walked in.

He scared the girl real bad, and he and the young man began fighting. Finally, the old man killed the young man and took him into a secret room that opened with a hidden panel. The girl ran crying into the room with her lover, and the older man put both of them in there and left them.

The traveler had hidden and watched the whole thing, then afterwards he went to the police and told them what had happened. They went to the house to investigate, and sure enough they pressed the panel and the door to the room opened, and in the middle of the room were two skeletons clasped in each other's arms.

The police told the man that the owner of the house had taken the young girl, who had been engaged to a young man that was real poor, and married her because her parents wanted the older man's money. Later, the young man had also disappeared, and they had heard that all three finally died.

Nobody ever found exactly what happened that night in the house, but the next year on the same day, the house fell down during a storm and hid its secrets forever.

Mary Kirk DeShazer, as told by Mrs. Trentice Head, Lewisburg, January 4, 1970. Courtesy of Folklife Archives at Kentucky Library, Western Kentucky University

Woman's Ghost Disappears

Logan County

I am familiar with the story about the Baylor ghost at the McCutty House near Oakville, Flintridge. It goes back to the Bank of Kentucky in Louisville, which issued money to the Baylors, but they lost their home when they couldn't pay the money back to the bank. Mrs. Baylor is supposed to be the ghost that haunts the place. She resents their changing the furniture.

Overton McCutty was sick one time, and woke up and saw a woman in gray at the dresser who was combing her hair. In that same room, one of the McCutty children, who was the niece of the bank's president, was nine years old and she was taking a nap. When she woke up, she wanted to know who the lady in gray was that woke her up.

On a number of occasions, she's been seen, although not recently. That was twenty or twenty-five years ago when these things happened. She's also been seen in the basement.

Louise Walker was going to be married, and she personally told me this. Her fiancé was being taken around the house to meet friends. When they turned in from the road to go up to the driveway, a woman was sitting on the porch, and she got up and went inside. When they got out of the car and knocked on the door, no one answered. Later the owners told them that the house had been locked and no one could possibly have been at home.

Mary Kirk DeShazer, as told by Mrs. Edward Coffman, Russellville, January 2, 1970. Courtesy of Folklife Archives at Kentucky Library, Western Kentucky University

Ghosts in Old Hotel

Christian County

One night I went to a hotel on Ninth Street in Hopkinsville, named New Central Hotel. I checked in at 3:00 A.M., and was met at the door by the hotel clerk. He had a heavy voice, the kind you would hear on a horror movie. He gave me a room on the second floor that had medieval features.

I found a sink at the edge of the bed, an old water heater, broken windows with stinking curtains, holes in the bedspread, and a fifteen-foot ceiling. I took my clothes off and laid down on the bed. I tried to sleep, but I couldn't. I heard footsteps outside my door all night, walking, walking, walking.

I saw someone peeping through my window, so I got up but no one was there. I then closed the curtains and laid down on the bed again.

But I couldn't sleep because of the water pipes. I kept on thinking then that I saw this thing come through the door, but the door was closed. Whatever it was had on a long red gown, had a long tail like a tiger, had horns, and a face like a Chinese mask.

I stayed up after that, and left about three hours later.

Don Lamar Owen, as told to Mary J. Oldham, Hopkinsville, 1972. Courtesy of Folklife Archives at Kentucky Library, Western Kentucky University

Little Girl's Ghost

Bullitt County

I was washing dishes and had this feeling there was someone watching me. I turned around and saw this little girl standing in the door. I said, "Who do you belong to?"

I thought she was a friend to this lady down here. She didn't say anything, just turned around and come straight through here. I followed her straight into this room, but by the time I got here she was gone. So I thought that little girl must have really been moving on!

Well, I didn't think anything about it the first time, because it didn't bother me too bad. But a few days later, I had that same feeling and turned around. This time, she was standing back toward the hallway. I asked her, "What are you doing?"

She never opened her mouth, but this time she looked straight at me, and the only thing different about her was that she didn't even look real. Her eyes were just blue! You know how it looks after a rain. That's the way her eyes looked. They were just as blue as could be.

So she came this way, and I went that way and said, "I'll head you off, little girl to see who you belong to. You're not scaring me."

By the time I got around, she wasn't there.

Mrs. James E. Creighton, as told to P. D. Pitchford, Brooks, 1978. Courtesy of Folklife Archives at Kentucky Library, Western Kentucky University

The Legend of Doc Wright

Bullitt County

There once was a man named Doc Wright, who owned a very large farm. He raised horses on this farm, but he would hardly ever sell a horse because he dearly loved horses. Well, being what he was, Doc got into some financial difficulty and went bankrupt.

One night Doc said he wasn't feeling well, and he told his wife, who was sitting in a chair reading a book, that he was going to bed. About fifteen minutes later, she heard two shots, and she rushed into the bedroom and found Doc covered with blood. The police said it was a case of suicide, and Doc was buried soon.

About three months later, a hired hand who had worked on the farm, was walking through a field when he saw Doc, or what looked like Doc, riding his favorite mare. He shouted to Doc, and when Doc looked around and saw him, he kicked his mare and took off running. The hired hand caught up with the horse in the next field, and it was just standing there grazing without a bridle or saddle.

About a year later, Doc's wife moved away to Lexington, but the hired hand remained in the county in which he lived. One night, the hired hand walked by the old house, which was boarded up and was not occupied. He heard a noise inside the house, took a board off the door, and walked into the house. Then he opened the bedroom door, and there in a chair sat Doc reading by an old lantern. When Doc saw him come through the door, he ran out the back door.

Since that happened, the ghost of Doc Wright has not been heard or seen again.

Ivy McBride, as told to Gary Reesor, Shepherdsville, ca. 1973.
Courtesy of Folklife Archives at Kentucky Library,
Western Kentucky University

A Haunted Bed

Jefferson County

This lady's husband joined the army, and she remained at home by herself. Every night, she would feel someone pulling the covers off of her.

She had a friend to stay with her one night. When she felt the covers being pulled off, she asked her friend there with her if she, too, felt the covers being pulled off. The girl thought she was playing.

The lady that lives there told her friend that it happens every night.

Jan Waddel, as told to David Rivers, Louisville, 1972.
Courtesy of Folklife Archives at Kentucky Library,
Western Kentucky University

Haunted House in Carbondale

Hopkins County

Roughly ten or fifteen miles from Earlington is a small town called Carbondale. Just before you reach Carbondale from Earlington, the road makes a sharp curve. Just past this sharp curve is an old gravel road on which you travel for several miles in order to get to the house. It is a two-story structure surrounded by several trees. The house is over a century old.

The story says that a man and his wife lived in it about seventy-five years ago. Of course, the house had no electricity, so the residents had to use oil or kerosene lamps in order to have needed light. Anyway, the man was a good bit older than his wife, who was about thirty at the time. But she had a lover, a country boy from that area. One night, the husband came home and found them upstairs in the bed together.

Naturally, he was pretty upset by the situation, so he began yelling threats and curses. The young man hopped out of a bedroom window, pants in hand. When he hit the ground, he ran under a large tree behind the house to put on the rest of his clothes. In the meantime, the husband strangled his wife with his bare hands and came running downstairs. He grabbed an axe and beheaded the young man right under the tree.

Today the house is in a run-down condition, and the tree is nothing but a stump. If you park your car in front of the house on a dark night, you can hear the wife's screams, see the dim coal oil lamps, and see movement in the upstairs window. The whole tree is visible in outline form, and something under it moves around.

No one has lived in the house for many years, and it is said there is no electricity.

Barbara Gaston, as told to Jim Francis, Earlington, 1972. Courtesy of
Folklife Archives at Kentucky Library, Western Kentucky University

Haunted Hospitals

Jefferson County

During the early years of the twentieth century, Louisville had the highest tuberculosis rate in the country; thus, a hospital was opened and named Waverly Hills Sanitarium for Tuberculosis. Many patients remained there until they died. Dead bodies were then pushed down tunnels to the bottom of the hill, where they were then carried off and buried. After the vaccine for tuberculosis was discovered, the hospital became a nursing home that is also now closed.

These days, an elderly woman may be seen running from the building with bleeding wrists and ankles. While doing this, she begs for someone to get her out of that place. Many have also seen people peeking out of the third floor windows. It is very spooky!

I am from Evansville, Indiana, and I remember there was an old abandoned tuberculosis hospital there that was supposed to be haunted. Many teenagers would go in and explore the terrifying hospital. There were needles, beds, and belongings that were left in the building for many years.

When I moved to Lexington, Kentucky, my friends and I were talking about haunted houses. And one of my friends, who is from Louisville, informed me about that old tuberculosis hospital in Louisville. I thought it was very interesting, because we had a haunted tuberculosis hospital in my hometown as well.

Courtney Oates, Bluegrass Community and Technical College,
Lexington, February 2008

The Boy of 5427

Jefferson County

It all started back in the summer of 1993 after my family and I moved into a new house. It was a nice five-bedroom house, with a pool in the backyard and a finished basement. It was not a house that you would expect to be haunted. It didn't happen on a dark, rainy night; it was actually a hot and humid night. My room was the biggest room in the basement. As a matter of fact, it was the biggest of all the bedrooms. I went to bed around 10:30 or 11:00 P.M. I had school the next day, as a junior in high school.

I was lying on my stomach in my bed, when for no reason my bedroom door creaked open. I looked toward the slow opening door and saw a shadow coming through the door. It was very dark down in the basement, as no light shined through the windows. I could only make out that it was small and childlike. So I thought it was my little brother.

As it made its way closer, assuming it was my little brother, I asked, "What do you want?"

I got no response and it got closer and closer. Still assuming it was my little brother, I wanted it to just get a little closer to me, and when he got close enough I could hit him in his leg or something, maybe a bad Indian burn. Patiently waiting for him to take one more step, there he was in range of a good frog to the leg. But as I hit where his leg would be, I hit nothing, nothing at all, just air. Then I got kind of nervous, but not overly scared. I put my head back down on the pillow but saw nothing. I laid there and listened, but heard nothing. I figured this would be my chance to run out of the dark basement, so I did. There were probably twenty steps leading from my basement room to the upper floor, and I maybe hit three on my way up.

The next morning, I told my mother that I wasn't staying in the basement any more, and then I told her why. She laughed it off because I was a big boy running from this childlike figure. After a few months of my sleeping upstairs on the couch, I decided to go back downstairs to a bedroom and stay. So I switched rooms, into the smallest room in the house. It had a small twin bed built into the wall; very small for someone who needed a lot of room space.

A few months went by with no sign of any boyish spirits running around. One night I was awakened in the middle of the night out of the blue. This time I was sleeping on my back when I looked down at the foot of my bed and saw a boy sitting at my feet. I looked at him, and he looked at me. We made eye contact. Like a kid, I pulled the covers over my head, but that didn't do any good. So I pulled the quilts back down, and he was gone. Back upstairs I went, sleeping on the couch for a good while this time.

Months and months carried by as I continued to sleep upstairs on the couch, or I sometimes made my little brother sleep on the couch and I would take his waterbed. I decided that the couch was for the birds, plus my mom kept yelling because the couch was new and I was going to, in her words, "break it down."

I told all my friends about this run-in I had had with the boy. Of course, like everyone else, they laughed and said I was crazier than they thought. So I started telling them, "Stay the night then." However, I couldn't promise it would happen that night.

In the summer of 1995 or 1996, my buddy across the street, Josh, lived in a house that had no central air. That summer, my mom and I asked Josh if he would like to stay with us that summer. When he decided to stay, I told him this would give him a chance to see the boy I was talking about.

A couple of weeks went by, still no sign of anything strange. But one night, the two of us were watching television in the basement. Josh was lying on the floor, and I was on the couch. We both had fallen asleep. Josh had turned off the television after I had fallen asleep. I woke up for no reason, then saw the little boy moving towards us. He wasn't walking, just gliding closer and closer. I whispered for Josh to wake up and that the boy was headed toward us. Josh raised his head, then put it back down on his pillow. I jumped up and turned on the ceiling fan lights, but the little boy was gone.

I asked Josh if he had finally seen the little boy. When he said no, I thought to myself that maybe I was hallucinating. The next morning he woke up, looked at me and said he had also seen it, but was too frightened to say anything. There, I had a confirmation besides myself.

The summer was coming to an end. It wasn't as hot at nights anymore, so Josh started staying back at his house again. It started getting a little cooler outside at nighttime, and on one occasion I was talking to a girl on the front porch of my house. I asked her if she'd like to go in and watch a movie or something. She said, "Yes, that will be very nice." Well, we went in and went downstairs and started watching a movie.

We started kissing and making out, then for no reason she stopped, then asked me, "What is that coming from the steps?"

I asked her what she was talking about, as I looked toward the stairs and saw a green bouncing ball coming toward us. It was bouncing and glowing. But as it bounced, it didn't hit the ground. The girl started putting her clothes on, tripping out. I got up, turned on the lights, and once more it was no longer there. The girl flew up the stairs quicker than I could ever imagine. She called me the next day and said she would never come in that house again, and she didn't.

That night was the last time I recall seeing anything. We moved out of that house in 2003, and my mom got terminal cancer and passed away. Then, my siblings and I put the house up for sale, and all of us moved into our new homes. But still to this day, I wonder if the boy at 5427 is still hanging out there, playing his games in the basement.

Dean Gregory, Jefferson Community and Technical College,
Louisville, February 2008

A Dream or Reality?

Knox County

This happened near my home in the Girdler area a few miles outside of Barbourville. I had personally seen, felt, and heard this thing. I was at my cousin's house, which was an older trailer at the base of a hill at the edge of a patch of woods. He lived alone there for awhile with nothing to contest his rest until one night when this happened.

His trailer always had a slight problem. At night, no matter how high he'd set the thermostat, it would always be a little chilly. On this particular night, he found out why. He lay there trying to get the sleep needed for school the next morning. But the trailer was a bit more eerie than normal; his sleep would have to wait. So, he decided he'd stare at the ceiling, hoping that boredom would form and he would become tired. As he lay there staring at the ceiling while in complete darkness, a strange gust flowed down his mattress. He continued to stare, then a figure flowed down, levitating like a mirror to him. It appeared to be a woman in her early to mid-twenties. Her hair waved with the gust and he continued to stare at her. She hovered closer and closer to him.

Fearing the worst, he remembered that having a Bible under your pillow while you slept would keep a ghost from being able to prove itself harmful until it had read the entire thing in one night. Reaching out in the darkness, he grasped the Bible he'd been reading the night before and placed it under his pillow, just as the ghost would have placed her hand on him. Now, with the Bible under his pillow, the ghost returned to its position hovering above him like a mirror. After a few moments, he fell into a slumber and woke up just before the alarm clock sounded. He'd wondered if it had been a dream, but underneath his pillow was the Bible.

A few weeks later, my brother and I were at this cousin's house and we saw instances that proved his theory of a she-ghost. She'd pass by us in a gust just as the sun would rest on the mountainside of eastern Kentucky's Appalachian Mountain range. And from time to time, you could see this she-ghost figure, feel the cold touch, or hear the slight noise of a footstep even though no one was moving.

On that particular night, we decided to get a few more people to come over for a get-together. So we went over and picked up some friends without telling them the theory. The night went by like normal until we all decided to go out to get something to eat. My cousin and I headed out first to start the car and prepare to leave, turning out the lights on the ends of the trailer, leaving the living room light on until everyone else left the trailer.

One of our friends came out next, leaving my brother and another friend to be last to come out of the house. Suddenly the bathroom light came on, showing a figure in the bathroom we could see from the car that was situated just a few feet from the trailer. There was a hustling sound, then the figure was gone. Then we heard a whooshing noise and thudding sounds, as though someone was running through the trailer. Seconds later, my brother and our other friend came dashing out of the house squealing. The friend slammed the door on the way out, but it didn't shut, just as if something was in the way of its closing.

I laughed and asked them if something was after them. My little brother's face proved what it was, but the friend was uncertain. He yelled while being out of breath. Continuing to smile, I walked cautiously up to the front door. Peering in as I grasped the doorknob, I smiled at the figure hovering just as my cousin had described her, then I slowly closed the door and rushed over to the car, feeling the eerie eyes of something watching me.

The day before my cousin decided to move out and leave for college, I had said that I wanted to stay in "her" room. In that particular room that had no windows, and the door always remained shut, we figured that's where the ghost stayed when it wasn't terrorizing us. I wanted to see what it felt like to stay in a room overnight with a ghost. Therefore, when that night came, and along with it that eerie chill, I headed into her room to spend the night.

I opened the door ever so slowly and crept into the dark room. The light flickered as I flicked the switch, and I saw a spot in the floor where I'd make my slumber. Moving a small box in the corner of the room, I lay down and went to sleep a bit too fast, especially since I was suffering from a rough case of insomnia at the time.

The dreams I had that night are too abstract, confusing, and gory to be put into words, except for the last scene. This "scene" was nothing more than a conversation with me and the she-ghost. She seemed as my cousin had described her: short, with long brown hair, and in her mid-twenties. She spoke to me softly about life and mainly the past. In the end, she said I would pass into the afterlife before most of my peers, but I would have a good life while it lasted. With this, I awoke.

A few hours later, my cousin said that he'd entered the room in the night to check on me and saw me curled up in the corner shivering and mumbling. To me, this all seemed more fake than anything, at least until news came the week after that happened that I had been diagnosed with a heart condition.

What I described took place in 2006.

Keith A. Swafford, Barbourville, April 16, 2008

The Visit to a Haunted House

Harlan County

Last year my daughter, Serena, decided to go visit her cousin. The family there did warn her about things that were, let's say, a little weird. There are four people that live in this house, including Annette; her husband, Jamie; and their two girls, Amber and Destiny. We have heard of their stories about how Destiny, at age four, had an imaginary friend named Hammie, and how Hammie was mean to her. Now, for a child her age, it is not abnormal for her to have an imaginary friend. However, it is abnormal that this friend was mean to her, and how Annette found Destiny sitting in the floor crying one day because she was in pain from Hammie pulling her hair.

When they first moved to this place, they tried to have a garden. Every day they would go outside, and there were always marbles in their yard. The more they dug up dirt, the more marbles they would find. Later on they found out that the family that used to live there had a little boy that would play with the child next door. The boy next door got a puppy one day and ran across the street to play but got hit by a truck, and both he and the puppy died. That family moved out and another family moved in—a lady with her husband and son. The man ended up going mad and killing himself in front of his boy. That family never moved, and still lives there today.

In the first few weeks of being there, Destiny's imaginary friend finally left, but more company came. Destiny was running into the kitchen to get some milk, and then all of a sudden she stops. Annette sees her do this and calls her over to see what was wrong. Instantly Destiny asked her mom, "Mom, who is that man in the jacket at the door?"

Annette gets spooked, so she goes to the door to see who it was, but no one was there. Annette's in-laws came in within the next couple of days, but she doesn't tell them about the man. Instead, Annette hears a story from them. Her mother-in-law told her about a man that came in their room, looked at them, left, and shut the door. A few other things happened, but I don't have time to tell it all.

Knowing of this, Serena still decides to go there to visit with them. During her first night there, she heard something in the house walking. She said she didn't see nothing, but felt someone watching her. She told Annette about her experience.

Later that day, she was sitting on the couch, and Annette comes in telling her to hurry and come in the bathroom, but not to let Destiny see her there. As Annette continued bathing her little girl, she starts asking her a question. She asked Destiny if her friend Kayla, another imaginary friend, was there last night.

"No," replied Destiny, "but her mom was here and she didn't like Serena being here for some reason. She's a little mean."

With that being said, both Annette and Serena got chills. Destiny continued to talk about how Kayla was coming over in a little while to play.

Several hours go by and they get more company. A little girl named Nevaeh and her brother Chris came by. Serena was watching them with Amber when Nevaeh went into Destiny's room. Serena then went to get her since she is only one, and when she went into the room, behind her a little girl ran by with a doll in her arms. When that happened, Serena picked up Nevaeh and ran out fast.

When asking Destiny about Kayla, Serena got a reply she didn't want to hear. Destiny described Kayla to Serena, and sure enough that was exactly what she had seen. Later that night, Serena also kept seeing the doll the little girl was playing with.

That was the first time Serena had ever seen a spirit, and she hasn't seen anything since, but I doubt she wants to see one again.

Billie Long, Harlan County, March 27, 2008

High School Prank Went Bad

Whitley County

In 1982 a group of high school students decided to participate in a senior skip day. They were going to play a prank on the other seniors. Five of the students went to an old high school building in London, Kentucky, and set up things they were going to do. Their first names were Michelle, Tony, Roy, Tracy, and Alex.

To get into their group, you had to go through one day of a haunted school! Well, the three kids, Joseph, Daniel, and Michael, that wanted to be in that group desperately followed the others up to the school. These three kids went in, but they never came back out.

Rumor has it that they went out the back door, but that all changed in 1983 when three bodies were found in the school building in a classroom. They were sitting in chairs in the front of the class. All that was left of them were their bones.

The legend behind the schoolhouse is that in 1978 a couple of students went into a killing spree and killed everyone, except one who was left to die in the classroom in which the boys were located. It is said that her spirit stays in that school because she is trying to find the people that did that to her.

In 1987, the school building was going to be torn down and made into a shopping center. But on the day of demolition, the school building burned to the ground. So they cleaned it up and built a shopping center within the first couple of months. Believe it or not, the shopping center burned down, so to this day nothing can be built there. Not even grass will grow on the spoiled ground, which means it is haunted ground.

Lisa Tennison, as told by Grandmother Wilma Moore,
Corbin/Bowling Green, May 26, 2008

Weird Happenings in House

Lewis County

When I was a little girl growing up, my grandma would always tell me tall tales about bizarre happenings involving ghosts and spirits that she personally encountered. Of course, this would scare me, but did I believe them? No, I didn't until one of them actually happened to me.

I was about seven years old and I was staying with my grandma. She would always tell me stories about how her house was haunted and, of course, I just shook them off. I mean my short attention span just couldn't hold on to the idea. It was nighttime (yeah, I know how all ghost stories start), and I was dying of thirst, so I got up and went downstairs. Everything seemed normal; nothing out of the ordinary going on. I got to the fridge to get some water, but then I heard a faint sound that seemed almost like a gasp for air.

I was startled, so I looked around to make sure that I was alone, and I was. I continued to get my water, but then there it was again. This time I could make out what was being said in a whisper of words. It was "Help please" that I heard.

By this time I was scared to death and didn't know what to do. So, I just slowly walked back to the stairs on the way, but on the way there I felt a brush of cold air along my back. I turned to see what it was, and there stood an outline of what appeared to be a little boy. It was there for only a second. That was it! I screamed at the top of my lungs and ran upstairs to my grandparents' room. I told my grandma of these bizarre happenings. She just smiled, then said, "I told you so."

The next day, all the happenings of that night were still fresh in my mind. I was trying hard to forget, but couldn't. I was still very scared. I hadn't slept any the previous night, so my grandma told me to take a nap, and I did. I slept for a good two hours, then woke up with a hard pressure on my chest. It felt as if someone was sitting on me. I tried to get up, but my arms were being held. Then I tried to scream, but no sound. Finally, I broke free and called for my grandma. When she came in she was surprised by fingerprints that were on my arm.

That was it. Me and my grandma did some research about the land on which she built her house. It turned out that long ago, a man who abused his wife and son committed a murder and suicide. He brutally held down his wife and suffocated her, while his son was on the phone with his friend whispering, "Help please."

Believe it or not, this is a true story.

Grandmother Norma Mason, as told to Whitley Mason,
Vanceburg, May 20, 2008

Ghosts in White and Brown Dresses

Logan County

My aunt lived in an old house at Keysburg. Her family didn't know there was anything the matter with that house. They stayed there a long time, but they went to bed one night. My aunt went to bed, and my uncle said, "You've got to get off of me."

They left and turned the light off. She said, "Elmer, I ain't on you."

He said, "You mashed me to death."

They had to get up and turn the light on because they couldn't sleep. They had to leave the light burning while they stayed there.

My aunt got up the next morning to cook breakfast. Of course, they'd get up early back then, before daylight. She had no wood in the cooking stove, and she came back from the table making biscuits, and the kitchen door was open.

She said there was something white that looked like a woman come in there and got in front of the stove like she was cooking, and stood there for awhile, then she went out the door.

My aunt said, "I just was in there."

She went on to say, "Directly, there was a woman come in there with a brown dress on. She stood up there in front of the stove."

She said that the woman in the brown dress went out, but didn't come back no more.

The next morning, my two cousins that were about fifteen years old was in the back room, and they had the window up. They were putting their shoes on in front of the old drape, and the same thing happened to them. [The woman in the white dress] went across in front of them, then went on through the house. Then they said that brown dressed woman crawled through the window.

They said they didn't know what it was. They never knew who the brown woman was. They didn't know nothing about the ghost, but they stayed there a long time and didn't let the ghost run them off.

James L. Pearson, Lewisburg, March 22, 2008

Murdered Woman's Ghost

Letcher County

This family in Jenkins, Kentucky, lived in a house where a man had beaten his wife to death. He then knocked her down the stairway but got so scared he hid her in the closet upstairs and covered her with rugs. Sometime after this happened, another family moved into the house.

Everything went just fine at first, but then some strange happenings took place, and they could see and hear things. It began to happen when they could hear something moan and moan in the closet. It would gurgle and moan, and finally scream. Then there would be a sound like someone falling down the stairs, and suddenly as it seemed to hit the bottom the whole house would shake.

People laughed at this at first because they felt it wasn't true until it happened during the day when someone would be there and see or hear it themselves.

Two different people saw a beaten, bloody-faced ghost come up over them and spread bloody, bruised arms out toward them. Then suddenly it would disappear. One boy became so scared in the house at something he saw, he went into hysterics and almost died. Various things like that have happened in that house.

The last I heard, they were going to tear the house down to see if they could find something, because the last family that lived there had a great shock. They went home one day and found their mother dead in the upstairs room.

This is supposed to be true. Ghost tales may really happen after all.

Diana Hester, location unspecified, 1969. Leonard Roberts Collection,
Southern Appalachian Archives, Berea College

Haunted House on the Hill

Whitley County

Robert L. Davis, his wife, and eight children moved from North Carolina to Tennessee in 1887 in a covered wagon. Before they reached their new home in Copper Hill they had a strange experience.

En route from North Carolina, they stopped in a community to spend the night. They saw a vacant house on the hill, then after inquiry they heard it was supposed to be haunted. Mr. Davis thought it would be a good place for the family to rest, so he paid no attention to warnings offered him, then proceeded to encamp there for the night.

After dark, the mother and children began to talk about the things that had been told to them about the house. Some of the children even got afraid, but the father kidded them. When one of them tried to shut a door, it would come open again. After doing this a few times, the father picked up a chair and placed it in front of the door as he laughed at their fears. But when he sat down, they looked to the door and saw it moving, chair with it.

Mr. Davis told his wife to get the baby and to take the children to the wagon. There they spent the remainder of the night, some distance from the house. During the night they saw lights flash on and off all over the house.

The next day, Mr. Davis saw a man who had warned him about the house. When he told him about their experience, he asked the man why the house was so strangely haunted. The man told him he did not know why, but that a woman had once lived there. She died in the house, and folks said that when she was dying, she cursed and climbed the walls.

Rosella Shaw, as told by Mattie Brown, Williamsburg.
Leonard Roberts Collection, Southern Appalachian Archives,
Berea College

Murdered Man's Ghost

Simpson County

This story was collected from a number of people around my home in Franklin. However, the most accurate account was probably from Mr. Blewette, who was in the immediate area at the time it happened.

About thirty years ago there lived in the house in which my family now lives, a woman, her son, and a colored hired hand. The son came in late from a ball game one night and cut the hired hand's throat with a hatchet. No one knows for sure the exact motive; however, the most popular one is that the son found the hired hand in bed with his mother.

This being a rural community, everyone was aroused, and several people gathered around the house within a short time. Mr. Blewette was one who was there. Immediately upon killing the man, the son took his shotgun and headed for the Robey swamp, which is located about a half mile from my home. He returned to his barn to sleep the next night and was apprehended. His plea of insanity got him sent to an asylum instead of a prison sentence. The boy is still living with his mother in the northern section of the county.

Some of the people in this community were a bit superstitious and believed that the man's ghost would haunt the house. Subsequently, in a short time all kinds of stories were floating around about the house being haunted. We heard these stories from neighbors within a short time after we moved in.

In the room in which the man was killed, blood is supposed to come up on the floor every time it rains. There is a swinging door between the dining room and kitchen which sometimes swings when the wind blows just right. Some think that this is the ghost. There are big mirrors over the mantels in some rooms, and car lights can be seen flashing in them sometimes as there are roads all around the house. This is supposedly another of the ghost's pranks. Other things such as the brushings of limbs against the house give ground for their ghost stories. One girl told me right after we moved there in 1946 that she wouldn't spend a night in that house for one hundred dollars.

Guy Simmons Jr., as told by J. F. Blewette, Franklin,
date unspecified. D. K. Wilgus Collection,
Southern Appalachian Archives, Berea College

Ghosts of Murdered Persons

McLean County

Somewhere around 1780 a new family moved to the Beech Grove neighborhood, not far from what is now Calhoun. The family consisted of the husband, wife, two infant children, and his brother, who was mentally retarded and who was subject to wild fits. The feebleminded brother was kept chained loosely in the attic to keep him from running away. He did not have enough intelligence to free himself, but was able to watch the children to see that they did not wander off while their father and mother were working in a nearby field.

One afternoon the wife came home from the field early in order to have her husband's meal ready for him when he came in. Upon arriving at the house she found that her mindless brother-in-law, in a mad fit, had beaten the children to death with his chains. Going completely berserk, she attacked him with an ax and killed him. Then, grieving over her children and what she had done, and being afraid of her husband, she hung herself in a huge oak in the front yard.

Upon returning home and finding his entire family slaughtered, her husband cast himself into a water well and drowned.

The frontier house stood unoccupied for many years. During this time, the old oak tree became a favorite hanging place for horse thieves.

Before long, people were afraid to come near the place, for it seemed that something bad happened every time someone came near it. A hunter was killed by a panther, and a young child fell in quicksand nearby.

Back during Prohibition, six moonshiners decided that it would be a safe place to hide a still because no one ever came around. They put the still in the barn behind the house, and one night as they celebrated a big moonshine whiskey sale, they began making fun of the "ghosts" that had been hiding them. As they joked, a fire mysteriously started at both ends of the barn and trapped them inside. One of the men, badly burnt, escaped the fire and lived long enough to tell what had happened.

Now their ghosts, the ghosts of the family, the hunter, and the little child, as well as the horse thieves, still haunt the old house.

Not many years ago, an elderly lady moved into the yet sturdy old house and spent one night. The next day her daughter came to visit her, but she found the old lady out of her head talking about ghosts. She is in an asylum now.

A little later, a family of five moved into the house, but at midnight the family moved their furniture out of the house and walked eight miles to spend the night with a neighbor. They have not been back to the old house since then.

Today the old house stands alone in a huge forest, and at night the wife can be seen walking through the house carrying a candle, which gives off a green light. As she walks she calls for her children, and the mad brother rattles his chains in the attic, and the children cry.

This story is believed by the people of this area and it is told as the gospel truth.

Allen Miller, as told by Faye Dever, Rumsey, 1961. D. K. Wilgus
Collection, Southern Appalachian Archives, Berea College

4

CIVIL WAR GHOSTS

~

Ghost of Confederate Soldier

Clinton County

My uncle, Jeff Phairs, was in high school at the time here in Clinton County when this took place. One night he was in his room about 12:00 midnight, or 1 o'clock in the morning. He was lying in bed staring at the wall when something walked into the room and sat in a chair located near the foot of the bed. They just stared at each other.

My uncle got out of bed and went to wake my mom, Katrina Phairs Collins, so she could come and look at this guy. He was dressed in a gray uniform with a sword. When my mom went into the room, the soldier disappeared.

We don't know who it was because Grandma's house was built over where another house was located in earlier times. In that old house, a guy hanged himself. They said the Confederate ghost looked like a Cooksey.

Beverly Phillips, Albany, 1992

Confederate Soldiers' Bloody Footprints

Cumberland County

During the Civil War, two Confederate soldiers were hiding upstairs in the Bob Armstrong place, located on Leslie Road. It is said that some Union soldiers came into this house and found the Confederate soldiers upstairs and killed them. They dragged the soldiers' bodies down the steps and buried them across the road in an old cemetery.

It is not known if family members living in that house were harmed or not. But people who lived in that house years later said when it rained, bloodstains would show up on the stairway. Every now and then, residents would hear something being dragged down the steps, so they would check it out, but nothing was there.

The house was torn down about three years ago, and the logs were sold to someone from Texas who supposedly built a B & B with the logs.

Michael Thrasher, as told to Olivia Brewington,
Burkesville, September 23, 2007

The Old Knocker

Metcalfe County

Howard Billingsley's house [that was located before it burned] here in Hickory College had in it what people back then called a "haint." Whatever it was sounded like something walking. I'd call it just a flat noise. We were over there one time and if I had heard it, but not expecting to hear it, I wouldn't have known what to think. It would have been something terrifying, but it wasn't. The Basil Sims family that lived there said, "There goes Old Knocker."

The noise was just like someone crippled going across the floor. But as far as it being anything outstanding, I didn't think anything about it. However, if I had heard it at night I would have been scared. Anyway, they said it just sounded like something rolling down the stairs, but when you'd open the door there wouldn't be anything there.

I've heard people say that someone was killed upstairs, and that the bloodstains were still on the floor. As far as who it was, or when it happened, I don't know. It seems to me that they did claim it was a soldier killed up there, or that a soldier had killed someone up there. So, I guess that old house was built before the Civil War.

Mrs. Cordie Glass, as told to Kay Harbison, Hickory College,
August 28, 1968. Similar versions were related by Ollie and
Tol Sartin, as well as Pearl Glass, August 28, 1968, Hickory College

The Galloping Horse

Morgan County

In Morgan County, where a hanging was stopped by Captain John T. Williams of Civil War fame, a horse and rider were heard for many years but were never seen.

A friend of the Captain, who sympathized with the Union, was being hanged. When Captain William heard about it, he galloped to the hanging tree to stop the hanging. Thereafter during the dark of the night in that area, a horse has been heard galloping out the Licking River Road, past the farmhouses, to stop suddenly at the hanging tree.

Frankie Hager, as told to Jim L. Clark, Owensboro,
April 10, 1969. Courtesy of Folklife Archives at
Kentucky Library, Western Kentucky University

The Lonely Grave

Nelson County

Only the last part of this story is known. The first part has been fashioned by probabilities that have been born of the War Between the States. It was in the year 1862, when the tides of the war were ebbing and flowing, first to one side and then to the other, throughout the battlegrounds.

At this time, there was found a lonely grave far away from the battlefield. Does a Confederate soldier lie there? Or did he wear the blue? Did his companions have time to utter a prayer as he was lowered into his grave far from home? Did they carry a last message to his mother or wife, his sister, or his sweetheart? No one knows. No one ever came there seeking a lost one.

In time, a house was built near the spot. It is a fact that for years the grave was decorated with flowers on Memorial Day. The children in the community had pity in their hearts for him who lay alone.

Years passed. And as long as the farm remained in the hands of a certain family, a large field rock was kept at the grave to mark it. The land went to another family of newcomers who did not know the story of the lonely grave in the field. The farmer burned his tobacco bed over the spot, not knowing what lay beneath. In the middle of the bed was a bare place the size of a grave, on which no plants, nor even weeds, grew.

To this day, nothing grows on the grave of a young man who died nameless.

Grace Snyder, as told to Anna Ruth Burgin, Bloomfield, 1959. D. K. Wilgus Collection, Southern Appalachian Archives, Berea College

Unquiet Mother

Knox County

This tale was handed down from the Civil War about Mrs. Webb and her son and a neighbor son. Mrs. Webb was a crippled lady in one arm, and she raised a son. This son of hers and the neighbor's son went to the army. The neighbor's son got back home safely. The Webb boy got killed and his mother heard about it. She took sick and died before the neighbor's boy got back.

One night the neighbor's boy was slowly riding past the old graveyard. Somebody called to him and he raised his head to see who it was. There stood a woman at the graveyard leaning on the fence. The moon was shining very brightly. She said, "Do you know anything about Jim? Did he get killed?"

The boy told her he got killed soon after they left. The woman said, "That's what I heard," and vanished away.

Eph Overton, as told to Melda Hall, Trosper, 1956. Leonard Roberts Collection, Southern Appalachian Archives, Berea College

The Haunted House

Magoffin County

About two miles from my home is an old, old house. It was supposed to have been there during Civil War days. Some very fierce fighting is supposed to have taken place near the old house. It's located near the mouth of Puncheon Creek on Route 7 in Magoffin County. Ever since I can remember, I've always been told the house is haunted. It is said that it is impossible for anyone to sleep in one particular bedroom. As soon as you go to bed, something puts cold fingers on your throat, and cover cannot be kept on the bed. It just rolls off on the floor, and if you try to get a look at the ghost, it goes up in the loft of the house.

The story claims that way back in early teens two old rich peddlers stopped at this house to spend the night. During the night, they were murdered and robbed in this bedroom, and the people who lived there say they knew nothing of how the murder happened.

They became so frightened they took up part of the floor and buried the two men under the bedroom floor, and ever since then this [ghost] thing has been there. The people who last lived there just nailed up that door and never used that room.

They say that nothing is seen or heard in the other rooms.

Virginia S. Holliday, location unspecified, 1960. Leonard Roberts Collection, Southern Appalachian Archives, Berea College

The Crawling Man

Barren County

This is a story I heard when I was a teenager. It was told to my mother by her friend Lucy Bray.

There was an old cabin here in Glasgow in which this old miser had lived for many years. Well, he died and this woman either bought it, or it was willed to her, and she moved in. Back then there wasn't any electric lights, or any modern heating systems. People used coal oil lamps if they could afford it, or candles and either wood-burning stoves or fireplaces. And this old cabin had a fireplace.

This woman moved in, and on the very first night as she went to bed she began to hear the most horrible groans and moans coming from the fireplace. Being scared to death afraid to move, the hair on her head would stand up, for out of the fireplace the dark figure of a man would come crawling to the foot of her bed. Then, it would return to the fireplace taking on something awful. This continued to happen every night, and by the end of the week she was a nervous wreck.

A friend of hers who happened by to see her was shocked at the way she had changed and, after some persuasion, got the woman to tell her what was going on. Her friend went on to tell her that if it came again that night get a Bible and ask it in the Lord's name what it wanted.

So that very night, as before, just as she laid down here comes the shadowy man out of the fireplace moaning and sounding terrible. The woman raised up and grabbed a Bible off her night table, and holding it out toward the figure, she asked it in the name of Jesus why it was bothering her. Slowly it turned and crawled back toward the fireplace, but before it disappeared, placed its hands on one of the old bricks, then pointed to her, and then back to the brick, and was gone.

The next morning, the old woman went to the fireplace and started removing the brick the creature had pointed to. Well, lo and behold, behind that brick were three bags of gold coins dating back to the Civil War. The woman was now pretty well off, no longer poor.

The crawling figure, which all her neighbors now knew, was that of the miser, who was never seen or heard again.

I don't know if this story is true, but my mother's friend told it as the truth.

David Allen Thomas, Glasgow, September 29, 2007

Ghost at Liberty Hall

Franklin County

During the Civil War, a young lady was left alone in Frankfort on her sizeable estate located next to the Kentucky River. Her husband had gone off to war, leaving her alone with only servants to care for her. She became seriously ill during this time, so she sent a message to her aunt to come over from West Virginia to care for her.

Everything was arranged for the aunt's stagecoach trip to Frankfort. On the way to Kentucky, her aunt also became ill and had to stay in bed somewhere between here and West Virginia for two or three weeks. When the aunt arrived in Frankfort, still a little ill herself, she found that her niece had died. Three months later, the aunt died in Liberty Hall.

From that day until now, many people living in the area of the house have reported strange happenings in the house. In 1964, a team of parapsychologists and a member of the National Historical Society went to live in the house for one week to record all strange happenings.

The people that lived directly across from Liberty Hall said that it wasn't unusual at all to be sitting on the front porch at night and see a candlelight go from one window to the next, upstairs and down. The parapsychologists claimed that at times at night, especially around the niece's room, they would see a grayish mist float through the halls and rooms, looking like fog off the river.

A story began to spread in Frankfort stating that when the aunt died, her soul was to remain in the house and take care of anyone that might stay there from then on. She had the weight of the uncompleted task of taking care of her niece, so she must stay there and care for others to come. They say that when you drive by at night and park in front of the house, sometimes you can see the candles going from room to room. It is said it is the aunt checking over the house to care for anyone in it.

When the legend of the Gray Lady, as she is now called, began to spread, Liberty Hall was historically known for its antiques and garden in the back, but became more known for the ghost in it.

The Historical Society has now made it into a museum where people can tour the house and garden.

Jim Crestman, as told to Molly Tuttle, Frankfort, April 14, 1973.
Courtesy of Folklife Archives at Kentucky Library,
Western Kentucky University

5

Roadside Ghosts and Odd Phenomena

~

Men Carrying Casket

Laurel County

Mamaw loved to tell ghost stories and sing scary songs as she played her guitar. She had many stories to tell and we never got tired of hearing them, especially this one.

"When I was a little girl around ten years old here on Spring Cut Road in Laurel County, we didn't have cars. Back then, wherever we went we had to walk or ride in wagons pulled by horses. One evening we were all going to church at a preacher's house. His name was Caleb Lee Moore. We were riding in a wagon with another family, the Helton's. There was about ten of us in all.

"It was getting dark and we had to take a road that went through the woods before we got to the preacher's house. Well, the wagon wheel got stuck on a tree stump, so we all had to get out of the wagon and wait for the men to get the wheel loose.

"All at once Mommy Scalf said, 'I want you all to look over there!'

"We looked and saw six men carrying a casket up the side of the hill. They had on dark suits and white shirts, and the moon was so bright you could even see the different ways these men combed and parted their hair.

"All of us kids started screaming and hollering and hanging on to our mommy's dress tails. All of a sudden these six men disappeared.

"Well, we finally got the wagon loose and went on to church, but boy did we all dread having to come back through them woods when it was time to go home. We were all afraid we'd see them ghost men again."

Eathel Scalf Henson, as told to Cindy Bailey, Barbourville, date unspecified

Hitchhiking Ghost

Monroe County

Back in the 1920s, the mail was carried by horseback along Star Route, which was from Tompkinsville to Summer Shade. It took all day and into the night to make the trip, and just over the hill below where I live, there was something that would jump up behind Mr. Smith onto the horse. It looked just like a man, and it rode to the top of the hill, then would jump off, Smith said.

Other mail carriers that rode horses on this route told this many times.

Jacob Curtis, as told to Robert Curtis, 1970.
Courtesy of Folklife Archives at Kentucky Library
and Museum, Western Kentucky University

Ghost That Wasn't a Ghost

Logan County

This guy was on the side of the road hitchhiking on a really dark night in the middle of a thunderstorm. Time passed by slowly and no cars passed by. It was raining so hard he could hardly see his hand in front of his face. Suddenly he heard a car moving slowly, approaching and appearing ghostlike in the rain. Whatever it was slowly crept toward him and stopped.

Wanting a ride really bad, the guy jumped in the car and closed the door. Only then did he realize there was nobody behind the wheel. The car slowly started moving and the guy was terrified, too scared to think about jumping out and running. This fellow saw that the car was slowly approaching a sharp curve, but still too scared to jump out of the car to run away since he felt sure the car would go off the road and into the marsh, thus slowly drown. But just before the curve, a hand appeared through the driver's window and turned the steering wheel, guiding the car safely around the curve.

Paralyzed with fear, the rider watched the hand reappear every time they reached a curve in the road. Finally, after taking all he could handle, the man jumped out of the car and ran into town. When he got there, wet and in shock, he went into a restaurant and, voice quivering, ordered a cup of black hot coffee, then told everybody his experience.

Everybody in the restaurant stayed quiet, but all of them got goose bumps when they realized he was telling the truth. About half an hour later, two guys walked into the restaurant and one of them said to the other, "Look Jethro, there's that idiot who rode in our car while we were pushing it when it was raining."

Brenda Lane, Auburn, March 13, 2007

Mysterious Phenomenon on Chestnut Ridge

Grayson County

I was taking Eddie up on the mule and let him off at the path. It was about three o'clock in the morning, and he told me I'd better watch out or I'd get thrown from the mule if that thing fell out of the tree. I thought he was just trying to scare me. I got around the ridge, and I did hear it fall out, about like it was coming down through the tree branches. It sounded like it was a man falling down through the trees. It fell down right behind my mule and rolled down through the woods like a big barrel. I never hear it in the same place.

Then me and Willard Langley was going up through there on a mule at the other end of the ridge, and we heard it falling down through the limbs, and it went rolling down the hill like a big barrel, just like the other one. It jarred the ground when it hit the ground. Arthur Langley has heard it, and Tommy Herle has heard it, and so has Wilbur Tilford.

If you went through there expecting to hear it, you never heard it. But if you weren't expecting to hear it, you always heard it. Another old man claimed that he'd heard it for years and years. I believe that the guy that shot that man off of my granddad's wagon-load of corn, and laid two flat rocks over his eyes, left the state but was never caught and arrested. But when he died, he told them that he'd killed that man.

My mother always claimed that my grandfather walked through that field and had the man working for him hauling loads of corn. And that guy got up in that tree and shot him off the wagon. It is said that man's eyes kept rolling around as he died. My mother said they took his bloody clothes and put them in an old suitcase after they dressed him and buried his bloody clothes out in the orchard. She was just a little girl then.

Preston Burnette, Leitchfield, March 1992. Courtesy of Folklife Archives at Kentucky Library, John Morgan Collection, Western Kentucky University

The Haunted Corner

Metcalfe County

Sometime back in time when we just had dirt roads, there was a corner on the road near Summer Shade. There was a tree near there, and on the tree was a branch on which a man had been hung, but none of the local people knew who he was or where he was from.

As the story goes, you could hear a shrieking sound when you came near the tree. Children would never go by there at night, and not even adults liked to.

This story was told to me by older people who said it was true. Believe it or not, the sounds were always heard on Halloween night when spooks were seen everywhere.

Rebecca Isenberg, as told by Lanos Isenberg, Summer Shade, 1969

John Neville's Ghost

Metcalfe County

This is a story about a ghost where John Neville was hung. There was a road that went through the woods over there. I've always heard it said that at night people would go by where Neville was hung, and when they got pretty close, a big ball of fire would rise up out of the ground. They'd just ride on by until they got past the dogwood tree where he was hung, then the fire would just disappear.

Local people have said the ball of fire was seen several different times.

Clayton Barrett, as told to Kay Harbison, Summer Shade, September 3, 1968

Ghostly Creature Frightens Mules

Monroe County

I'll tell you what me and Fred Rasner done. This is about the first ghostly thing I ever did see. Me and poor old Fred seen this. At that time, Will Jackson was making me a moonshine still. And let me tell you, he could really make a still, back when I used to follow that kind of business. Well, we rode these mules of mine and went over to Jackson's house in the middle of the night.

We got over around Wood Dunham's place, located close to the Rich Dunham Cave. I God, when we got to the cave, one of my mules just turned around and started snorting. Whatever it was was flying, and believe me it was. So here comes Fred Rasner after me. He said in a real slow voice, "What did you see?"

I told him, "I God, I don't know. I never seen anything, so let's go back." Then I said, "I can't do nothing to help this mule."

Well, we liked to have never got our mules back down there. All of a sudden, this thing went walking across the road real slow. Well, that Fred Rasner got down off that mule and started looking for a rock!!! Then he said, "Jim, I can't find nothing."

I said, "Get up from there. They ain't no telling what that thing is."

About that time, my mule swirled around again, and Fred's started swirling, too. We finally got them started back to Will Jackson's house. When we got there and then started back home from Will Jackson's, I had that big thirty-gallon still up in front of me on the saddle. Right along about there, our mules seen it again, whatever it was. Now, you never heard such a racket coming up that road in all your life. It scared them mules to death.

Fred wanted to go back that night to see what it was all about. What we seen was the only thing I ever seen in my life. It was black, just right black, and a very big thing. We never did figure out what it was. That's the only ghostlike thing I ever seen in my whole life. It might not have been a ghost, but to us it was.

Jim Bowles, Rock Bridge/Forkton, 1974

Ghost Crossing the Road

Butler County

This story is a firsthand account. In the winter of 1967, the night of our high school's homecoming basketball game, my best friend and I had gone into town that evening, and, of course, it was very dark as we started home. We lived about ten miles out of Morgantown in rural Butler County, and we were about halfway home when we came to a place in the road that topped a hill and also had a curve at the same spot.

My friend was driving her dad's new red Mustang, and just as we topped the hill she slammed on the brakes of the car and I let out a scream simultaneously. We both had one thought—we were about to run over someone. Just as we topped the hill, it looked like someone stepped out in front of the car. My friend had locked the car up, and there we sat in the road. No one was there but us. We both looked at each other and both exclaimed what we thought had happened; that is, we were about to hit a person who had stepped in the path of our car, only there was no one else around.

On the way home from there, we were amazed at what we had both seen, what we KNEW we had seen. At the time it happened, we had no thought of ghosts or apparitions, just the fact we were about to be involved in an accident.

We soon arrived home safe and sound, and my friend went back over this same road to the basketball game later that night. This was many years ago, and still when we get together we frequently refer to that night and remain convinced of what we saw and what happened the night of our homecoming basketball game and the ghost in the road.

Connie Embry, Roundhill community, December 16, 2007

Ghost Sitting by Tree

Monroe County

Back around 1915, when Dad and I were sitting around the fireplace, I decided to go see my brother some three miles away. My father said, "If you are going, take his guitar back." So I picked it up and started out.

I had to cross a dark hollow, and after crossing the hollow there was a road on the ridge. So I was thumping on the old guitar when I looked up the road some forty or fifty yards and saw a man sitting by a tree looking toward me. When I got close, I spoke but he was still looking at me and no answer was returned. Well, I went to the other side of the road but kept my eye on him. As far as I could see, he was still looking at me.

I told an old man about what I saw, and what tree it was at. He said that the tree was the one that Johnny was leaned up against when they carried him out of that dark hollow, waiting on a buggy to arrive to take him home.

Johnny was killed while cutting timber, and was dead when they carried him out and set him against that tree.

I've gone back there several times but never saw him again, but others say they have.

Jacob Curtis, as told to Robert Curtis, Tompkinsville, 1970.
Courtesy of Folklife Archives at Kentucky Library,
Western Kentucky University

Drowned Man's Ghost

Graves County

There's a legend that says at a certain stretch of Mayfield Creek the ghost of a man that died while crossing the creek years ago still haunts the creek. One day a man went hunting for rabbits near there and decided to cross the creek.

While he was on the bank, something grabbed him by the shoulders and jumped on his back, then commanded, "Carry me across!"

He didn't bother to look back because he was too scared. After he crossed the creek and the thing got off his back, the man then looked around and saw a ghost that looked just like the man who had drowned there.

Dana Elliott, as told to William Deaton, Mayfield, 1972.
Courtesy of Folklife Archives at Kentucky Library,
Western Kentucky University

The Ghost of Hebron Lane

Bullitt County

There is a small bridge in the middle of Hebron Lane, located north of Shepherdsville, Kentucky. Late at night you can see the ghost of Hebron Lane walking along the bed of the creek below the bridge. There is a small patch of fox glow below the bridge which shines during the night. The ghost walks to and fro beneath the bridge as if he were guarding someone, or something.

Many people crossing the bridge late at night do not linger long around the bridge. Others have stopped along the bridge to catch a glance of the ghost.

One account which comes to mind is that late one night a group of boys were crossing the bridge when they heard a rustling of leaves under the bridge. At first, they looked to see if it were a deer, or some other animal walking in the brush. Instead, they saw a ghostlike figure walking along the banks of the creek.

Not knowing what to think, the boys stood in amazement watching. The figure glanced up at them and gave a signal for them to come down to the creek. Being of a curious nature, the boys started walking down the bank to greet the figure. When they reached the bottom of the creek, the figure had disappeared.

The next day, the boys returned and looked for traces of shoe prints, but found nothing.

Ivy McBride, as told to Gary Reesor, Shepherdsville, 1971.
Courtesy of Folklife Archives at Kentucky Library,
Western Kentucky University

Dressing Up Weirdly

Crittenden County

My daddy had a brother-in-law that lived right across over here. He was married twice, first to an Oliver. They were working on some ground way back on a bluff over there. And there were some boys over there that believed in haints and ghosts. Well, this fellow and his wife fixed up a big tale and told these boys that they had seen a ghostly man over there on an old dying tree. It is said that people used to clear off new ground and deaden all the big trees, and cut all the little ones out. They would let them old trees stand there for maybe several years and cut them down for wood, and make rails out of them. Well, the bark would get loose on the old dead trees, and rot. Big black bugs would live under the bark.

They said they had seen a black man over there, and he would take a pole and punch the bark off the trees. When he did that, these bugs would fall to the ground, and he ate them. That's what he was living on.

Well, they had a field right close to this new ground and they was working on the other side of it. So they got a great big tall boy and put an overcoat on him, along with an old hat. Then they blackened his face and sent him over there. He would punch up a tree so that the bugs would fall out, then he would get down like he was eating them. Then they took their mules out and went home.

They said that they each one had a pistol that they carried in their hip pockets, and the plows wore blisters on their hips. They were back at work one day, and there was a boy that come through going over here to the Frances community to get some groceries.

Well, they was about a mile from where they was at work, and said that his brother-in-law said that we'd get some fun out of that boy, and that he'd dress up like that wild man. It had got out all over that country about that wild man, and he went to a stump and got charcoal off of an old stump that had been burned, then blackened his face.

And he got himself a pole and got behind a big tree there right close to the pass, and said that boy came along and he just walked behind like a ghost and warped the ground and scowled right loud. That boy took off, and just throwed his groceries as he ran away.

Well, they saw they had done the wrong thing, as he was just screaming every breath, so they took out after him. They chased him for half a mile before they ever caught him. When they caught him, they held him and he knew both of them after they told him who they was.

Well, they went back and helped him pick up his groceries and put them back. Then they gave him fifty cents apiece to not tell his father and mother about what they had done. It cost them a dollar, afraid they would get in trouble.

When they all got together, they could tell and do some of the doggonedest things!

Ali L. Whitt, as told to Michael McDonald, Frances, May 4, 1973.
Courtesy of Folklife Archives at Kentucky Library,
Western Kentucky University

Dead Body Causes Changes in Creek's Course

Lawrence County

Back when I was a lot younger, a man's wife disappeared. Nobody around here knew what had happened to her until about a year later. She was found then, and had been killed by her husband.

Her husband killed her one night when they were fighting, then he took her out and buried her. This would have been okay, but all the dogs in the country kept coming around and digging where she was buried. He decided after that to put her body where no dogs or anything else could find her. So he buried her under the creek.

After she was buried, the creek changed its course and left the spot where he had buried her as part of an open field. Because he was sure of what he had done, he never went back to check the spot where he had buried her.

The next spring, a farmer who tended the field was plowing it, and he found her body. After they took the body out, the creek changed its course again and flowed where it was supposed to.

Clyde Childers, as told to Isaac Hinkle, Cherryville, November 1973.
Courtesy of Folklife Archives at Kentucky Library,
Western Kentucky University

Talking to a Dead Man

Edmonson County

Charley Meredith had started to work I guess. About halfway to work, a man came out into the road with his team of mules. Charley spoke to him, and they talked for a few minutes, then Charley went on the way, and the other man went on his way.

Charley turned around and looked back, but the man was gone. Uncle Charley happened to remember that this man had been dead for several years. He knew that this man was dead, and remembered when he died.

Bertha Houchin, as told to Gary Watt, Chalybeate community, 1972.
Courtesy of Folklife Archives at Kentucky Library,
Western Kentucky University

Horses Recognized Murder Spot

Edmonson County

I remember hearing about when a man was murdered right down here at the foot of the knob near the Edmonson-Warren County line. The body was found behind a big rock by the road.

A neighbor was arrested and tried for the murder, but they turned him loose because there wasn't enough evidence that he did it. A little later, he died, and on the way to the graveyard they had to pass by the spot where the body had been found.

They were hauling the body in a horse-drawn hearse, and when they got to the spot where the body was found, the horses stopped and wouldn't go on past it. They beat the horses, but the horses would not go past that spot. They had to turn around and go on another road to get to the graveyard.

Everybody thought that the suspect had really been guilty after that happened.

Bertha Houchin, as told to Gary Watt, Chalybeate community, 1972.
Courtesy of Folklife Archives at Kentucky Library,
Western Kentucky University

Murder Spot

Edmonson County

Up where we lived, these two men got into a fight. They were both on horses a few days after that. One man was going one way, and the other man was going the other way. When they met, one of these men had a butcher knife and he reached over and cut the other guy's head off.

It is said that where this man's head hit the ground, the land never gets dirty. It looks like its been swept all the time. A leaf won't drop on it and grass won't grow on it. It is just a small sunken down, bare place in the ground.

Bertha Houchin, as told to Gary Watt, Chalybeate community, 1972.
Courtesy of Folklife Archives at Kentucky Library,
Western Kentucky University

Girl's Bloodstains

Lawrence County

One night several years ago, a girl was walking home from church. She saw a strange man walking behind her, so she hurried on. He caught up to her and robbed her, then hit her with a rock. She died from the lick with the rock.

It was several hours before she was found, because there wasn't any traffic on that road after eight o'clock. She had bled quite a lot from the rock that hit her, and it left a stain of her blood on the pavement. This ghostlike stain stayed on the spot on which she fell until the road was blacktopped a few years later. Now, her stain can no longer be seen.

Clyde Childers, as told to Isaac Hinkle, Cherryville, November 1973.
Courtesy of Folklife Archives at Kentucky Library,
Western Kentucky University

Woman's Death Spot

Lawrence County

Riding horses was the only way people could get around on Nats Creek. When people walked, some of their paths would only be used by maybe one person within six months.

One fall, an old woman was walking down Stone Cove on the way to her cousin's house, because she wasn't able to stay by herself during the winter months. Apparently she fell and hit her head on a rock, but no one was ever sure how she died.

When she fell, she rolled down into the hollow below the road, and her body wasn't found until the next spring. When it was found, it was laying on bare dirt with nothing growing on it. This spot is still bare, and weeds or nothing else is said to grow on it.

Clyde Childers, as told to Isaac Hinkle, Cherryville, November 1973.
Courtesy of Folklife Archives at Kentucky Library,
Western Kentucky University

Ghost at Middle Bridge

Warren County

The legend of this ghost states that the ghost appears during a full moon at midnight on Middle Bridge, which crosses Green River.

I was present at midnight during a full moon at this place, along with five other witnesses. One person noticed the moonbeams concentrating on a tree stump. We all looked and saw the light getting brighter and appearing to move toward the windshield of the car. Everyone in the car left right then, except myself, being as I was in a mild state of shock and could not get the door open.

Well, I got a pretty good description of the image, since it was within four feet of the front of the car. When I managed to get it together enough to split the scene, I ran [as fast as I could to get away from there].

What I saw appeared to be a transparent blue-white mist with the face of a young girl. I never saw that ghost again, although I have looked for it several times when the moon was full.

I had five witnesses to this happening, and I firmly believe that what I saw was a ghost.

Russell Miller, as told to Mike Brannik, Louisville, May 1972.
Courtesy of Folklife Archives at Kentucky Library,
Western Kentucky University

Ghostly Train Wreck

Logan County

This is a story about a train on a three-mile stretch near Oakville, here in Logan County. It is said that if you go to the three-mile stretch, which is now a paved road, but used to be a train track, and you turn off your car lights, you will see the train coming at you.

I'm not sure that I personally believe this, but I do know that I have seen it. That happened one night when my friends and I went down there just to see what we could see. Well, I'll kid you not, we all saw the train coming, but we are still in denial of what we saw. When we saw whatever it was, we turned our lights on and got out of there really fast.

This site is where a train wrecked a long time ago with a lot of people on it, and they all died in the accident. While we were there, we also smelled a really putrid odor when we saw the train.

Linda Howard Perez, Bowling Green, February 11, 2008

Murdered Woman's Ghostly Scratches and Screams

McCreary County

McCreary County is located in southeast Kentucky on the Tennessee border within the Daniel Boone National Forest. One of the poorest counties in Kentucky, McCreary suffers from lack of adequate law enforcement, in part due to the fact there is little private property available for taxing, but also because of the dense forest area. Regardless of the reason, criminal activity has been able to thrive for many generations.

In the late 1960s, a tale was told about a local resident, whose name I won't identify. Anyway, he had been visiting a family in Florida. While there he picked up a new lady love and brought her home for a visit. The sale of liquor was, and still is, illegal within the county, but that doesn't mean it is not readily available if one knows where to look. There are many unpopulated places in which to drink in relative peace. One such place is on Stephens Farm Road in Pine Knot, a small town in the southern part of the county.

Stephens Farm Road is sparsely populated, with the long, winding road ending at Wilson Cemetery. One cold, rainy night, just north of the cemetery, several men had gathered to drink and were joined by this man and his lady friend. Others that were present later said, without any words of warning, this man simply took a shovel from the back of his jeep and struck the unsuspecting lady across the back of her head. He buried the lady in a shallow grave in the very spot she fell. Those present who saw him kill her later said that he had struck her with enough force to knock the eyes from their sockets. Fearing this man's legendary temper, the crime was never reported. The unfortunate woman still rests in her unmarked grave; or perhaps not.

It is said today, when the night is at its darkest, and rain falls from a black sky, if you are parked in the clearing on Stephens Farm Road, you will hear a scratching on the back of your vehicle. The scratching will continue down the side of the car next to where you are sitting, and will end at the front fender of your car. While you are sitting wondering what the scratching is and seeing nothing, a woman will jump at your window.

Her screaming is horrible and any words are indistinguishable. She appears very angry and agitated beyond description. Her blonde hair is frizzy and her clothes are dirty. Her eyes are as big as saucers, with a gray light emitting from the empty sockets. It does not matter if you are alone or with others, when the conditions are right, she will come to you. However, once someone has seen her, they never see her again, because they refuse to return.

I do not watch scary movies, nor do I watch *Unsolved Mysteries*. I do not listen to ghost stories, and I would never investigate one to validate truth or fiction. It is not merely that I do not believe; it is that I do not want a reason to believe. I have no way of knowing if this story is true, but I do know the truth of an amazing coincidence.

About two years ago, a man was drinking in a bar across the Tennessee border, roughly three miles from this very location. On his way driving home, his vehicle was forced from the road and he was driven to this very spot described on Stephens Farm Road. He was robbed and then shot to death by two brothers. The last name of these two brothers was the same as that of the man who killed this woman.

Perhaps the ghostly woman has found company at last.

Deborah Gilreath, Somerset Community College, February 8, 2008

Car Lights That Weren't

Logan County

[As my father tells it,] "We lived in Keysburg, located in southwestern Logan County, back when I was small, let's say about eight years old. There was a stump and an old dirt road to this house located a pretty good piece away. At 8 o'clock at night in the summertime it would be dark. Me and my older brother was standing out there, and we saw a car and thought it was coming to the house. We just thought it was a car. So, the next night it done the same thing.

"Guy, my brother, said that it couldn't come around, but it [what we thought was a car] would hit the stump. I mean, it surprised me and him both. It lit the yard up, so we went down there and we couldn't find nothing.

"We didn't know what to think about it, except the car couldn't turn around because of a fence row on one side and a big field on the other. It had to come to the house to turn around. That was a ghost-like thing."

Pa said that the house was located at the dead end of a driveway. When the car would get to the stump every night, the lights would go out and the car just disappeared. Pa said this scared him and my uncle to death, and they ran to their mama and she said, "What's wrong with you boys? You look like you have just seen a ghost."

They said to her, "We did." They told her what happened, and the family moved shortly thereafter.

James L. Pearson, Lewisburg, March 22, 2008

Ghost of Young Bride-to-Be

Laurel County

There are many types of ghost stories about strange, unexplained mysteries, unknown visitors from beyond, and others like that that have always had people in wonder. The story I'm about to tell takes place in Laurel County. It is rumored to this day that a young woman walks the woods in search of a life she wanted, but never had a chance to have. She is known as the ghost bride, but her real name was believed to be Ann Smith. She was a young woman who had big plans for her future and life back in the early 1900s.

She was born and raised here in Kentucky, and her lifelong dream was to have her family to just love having a big country style wedding, with friends and neighbors and loved ones all by her side. As a young girl, Ann would play dress-up by putting on a white handmade dress from her mother's cedar hope chest, and she would dance around the room so happy and carefree. She dreamed about the day she would walk the aisle to get married to her true love, and that's what makes this story so tragic.

When Ann was sixteen years old, she felt she was ready to marry her childhood sweetheart, and after a few talks with great pleading, she finally received her parents' blessing. She wanted to get married on her upcoming birthday, September 7.

Her mother and sisters hand made a beautiful wedding dress, and when it was complete and she first saw it, she started crying with great joy. Her wedding dream was coming true.

Family members and other people started gathering together at Ann's home to walk to the church. To do this, they had to walk along a wooded trail along a dirt road that led to a pond where wild flowers and roses grew. Ann and her mother were the only ones left at the house, so they started on their walk to the church. Ann told her mother to go on, since she wanted to go by the pond and pick some wild roses and flowers to hold as she walked to the aisle.

All the people, along with Ann's family, waited for Ann to arrive, but after a little while they began to get worried because she hadn't shown up yet. Some of the men, along with her father, said, "Let's go check on her." So they went down to the pond where her mother said Ann was going to pick the flowers.

A great shock came upon all of them when they walked up and found Ann lying there lifeless with wild roses she had picked laying alongside her body. She had slipped on the rocks beside the pond and died instantly on the spot in her beautiful wedding gown.

It is reported to this day that on September 7, along any stretch of woods, you can still see her walking on her way to the wedding. Just last year on September 7, 2007, she was spotted by some fox hunters in a space of woods. They described what they saw as an eerie sight of a woman running through the woods barefooted with wild roses in her hand. The men said at first they thought something was wrong, so they ran to help the young woman they saw running, but she disappeared into thin air. And to prove the men weren't imagining things, they found seven rose petals laying on the ground.

There have been more sightings and unexplained things that people have seen and told about relevant to the ghost bride in the woods of Laurel County. Some say it is just a story, or an old wives' tale, but who knows. It may indeed be the ghost of the young bride-to-be.

Jonathan Lawson, London, April 14, 2008

The Haunted Tunnel

Bracken County

Legend has it that many years ago this particular tunnel became haunted by the ghost of this particular woman and several younger children. One evening several young children were playing in their grandmother's yard located near a drive-through tunnel, while the grandmother was in the house doing whatever it is that grandmothers do, such as cooking, cleaning, and so on.

All you could hear was the laughter of the children. Then in a moment's time, silence arrived and the act of the children was like something unthinkable. The children tied their grandmother up and dragged her from the house to the tunnel that was near the house. When they arrived at the tunnel, they placed a noose around her neck and hung her, killing her instantly. No one knows why the children took this action, or how they even planned it.

On foggy nights, they say that the grandmother returns, with the children's shadows and sounds wandering all around. It has been told that if you step outside of your car when the ghosts are near, you will fall to your knees and pass out.

In my own experience there, it was one that was deeply scary. While sitting in a parked car in the middle of the tunnel in dead silence, you could hear the laughter of those children all around. In the rear of the car you could see the shadows of the children jumping off the hillside down into the middle of the tunnel and walking toward the car, with the cracking of the sticks all around, as if you were to be their next victim to be attacked.

While there, the grandmother was never seen, but I wouldn't doubt but what she was there.

Brandon Pierce, as told to Ashley Clark, who also personally experienced what is described, Augusta, May 20, 2008

Ghost of Slick Rock Curve

Pike County

Slick Rock Curve gets its name from the rocks in Shelby Creek, located on U.S. 23 just north of Dorton, here in Pike County. On a very dark night is when the ghost appears, and it is a very friendly type ghost. It will walk along beside you and never touch you.

My cousin is the one who told me about seeing the ghost. His name is Jimmy McPeek and he lives in Michigan at the present. He was on his way home from a ball game one night, and was riding a bicycle. He said he heard some laughing as he came through the curve. It was a very dark night and sort of a scary one. He said he looked to his right and there the ghost was, big as life. He figured he could run faster than he could pedal the bike. He was scared badly by this time, so he started to run. He threw the bicycle on his back and away he went, with the ghost right beside him.

He had about two thousand feet to go to get home. On his way, he jumped a six-foot fence with the bicycle on his back and the door-facing tore it from his grip. He told his story, and to this day he has never walked through that curve.

The ghost is supposed to have been seen by some more people in the community.

Roger McPeek, as told by Jimmy McPeek, location unspecified, 1970.
Leonard Roberts Collection, Southern Appalachian Archives,
Berea College

Legend of Howard Branch

Magoffin County

There is something to be seen at the mouth of Howard Branch. I have heard this all my life from my parents, uncles, aunts, and cousins. Everybody always talked about the great hairy thing with the long claws.

The story goes that Buddy Arnett, who was a young man at that time, was acting mean by doing things he shouldn't do. There lived another man known as old Faby, who lived at the head of Lead More Branch. Faby made apple brandy and there was a crowd of mean people always there.

So Buddy Arnett had started up there when this thing jumped on his horse, then on his back, nearly choking him and scratching him. He told how he tried to shoot it with his pistol, but he couldn't hit it. It rode with him until he came to the mouth of Howard Branch, then jumped off and disappeared.

Well, Buddy went on to Faby's and was almost killed that night. Somebody hit him on the head with a club and left him for dead. He finally recovered and told this story.

As long as he lived, he claimed to have seen this thing, but no one else could tell what it was.

When riding horseback to a party on a moonlight night, everyone gave their horse a warp and dashed madly across. If cousin Tom was in the crowd, he took the lead, closing his eyes until he was at a safe distance.

When Buddy died it was said that the creature changed to a beautiful woman who dressed in white and walked along beside the rider, then disappeared at the mouth of Howard Branch.

Luna A. Howard, location unspecified, 1959.
Leonard Roberts Collection, Southern Appalachian Archives,
Berea College

6

Headless Ghosts

~

Looking for Missing Body

Owen County

My grandfather always told this story, and insisted that it happened on the L&N Railroad. It happened when two lovers had a quarrel and the girl ran off onto the ridge of the hill and the boy went after her with a flashlight when he met his unfortunate death.

The L&N Railroad was going along this ridge right outside of town, and the brakes on the train's back cars locked up. The engineer stopped to let one of the crew members get off to go back and release the brakes. And while he was working on the couplings between the cars, the train took a sudden lurch forward and his head was severed by the impact.

His head rolled off over the deep ravine and hit the lantern and knocked it over also. The head was never found, and at night you can still see the head and the lantern looking for the rest of the body.

Charles Alexander, as told to Dana Anglin, May 27, 1965. Courtesy of Folklife Archives at Kentucky Library, Western Kentucky University

A Staggering Ghost

Lawrence County

During the twenties and thirties, the railroad kept small cabins along the railroad line equipped with telegraphs so as to relay news of breakdowns, bad tracks, and general trouble to the work crews. During the night, these cabins were occupied by one telegraph operator, who usually didn't have anything to do but sleep or drink.

J. B. Cabin, which is on the road between Richardson and Patrick on the C&O Line, was cared for by an operator who seemed to like to drink more than sleep. One night he had an extra large supply of fresh whiskey, so he ended up a little drunker than planned.

He stumbled out of the cabin, then passed out on the tracks. A train run over him, tore him up pretty bad, and even cut off his head. Now, it is said that on certain nights he can be seen staggering of the tracks between Richardson and Patrick, looking for his head, which was never found.

Mrs. Bell Fitch, as told to Isaac Hinkle, November 1973.
Courtesy of Folklife Archives at Kentucky Library,
Western Kentucky University

Head Returns with Golden Ears

Pulaski County

One time there was a man that had worked on a railroad crew for years and years. He kept growing harder and harder of hearing until finally he was almost totally deaf, but he kept on working. One time he was working on a track when an unscheduled train flew up the tracks behind him. One of the old [black men] hollered for him to get out of the way, but, of course, he couldn't hear him. The train hit him and completely cut off his head. It rolled down the bank into a big pond. Twenty-five men tried to find his head in the pond, and even ten of these men saw it roll in there, but still couldn't find it. So they just buried him without a head.

Then, on the night he died exactly one year later, his wife woke up in the middle of the night because of a noise in the room. Then she saw her husband's favorite rocking chair rocking, and in the seat laid his head. But that's not all; his ghost head had big golden ears!!

Lloyd Godby, as told to Janice Simmons, Science Hill, November 1972.
Courtesy of Folklife Archives at Kentucky Library,
Western Kentucky University

Railroad Headless Ghost

Bell County

Once there was a big two-story yellow house near the mouth of a big branch near the Chad Railroad Yard. When I was a child, I was always afraid of this big old house because I had always heard so many haunt tales about two-story houses.

Uncle Chad Nolan lived in this big house, and his wife was dead. He lived there all alone. There was a woman that lived nearby that would come in and clean up his house and cook for him. Uncle Chad got killed on the Chad Railroad Yard one cold, drizzly day in December, just before Christmas. He was about eighty years old when he got killed.

There were seven long tracks through that railroad yard besides the main line and what they called a house track. There were three or four L&N boarding cars that were set off of the wheels to be used for the depot and freight house. Uncle Chad got killed about two hundred feet below the depot car, or to be a little more precise, just about halfway to his house from the depot.

The L&N passenger train was scheduled to pass through there every night at 8:45. Now, just after this train would go up on a rainy, drizzly night, there could be a man with no head walking up and down the railroad tracks.

Uncle Chad was a wealthy old man and he owned a lot of property all up and down the railroad tracks. It was thought by some of the early settlers that the headless ghost was trying to tell them where some of his money might be hid, or maybe something about his will, or some of his property. The headless ghost was just about the size man that Uncle Chad was, and he was drawn over as though age may have caused him to be drawn.

He walked with a walking stick just like the one Uncle Chad used when he was poking up and down the railroad yard.

Henry Pratt, as told to Betty Cusick, location unspecified, 1956.
Leonard Roberts Collection, Southern Appalachian Archives,
Berea College

Headless Man Messes with Flowers

Jefferson County

Two women were walking through the woods on their way to a church program. They were taking with them some pies in boxes covered up with flowers. A man with no head, who was dressed up in a tuxedo, was standing at the side of the path. He reached out and messed up the flowers on one of the ladies' boxes.

The other lady, the one who didn't see what happened, asked her what happened to the flowers.

The other lady said, "Didn't you see the man in the tuxedo back there? He did it."

"No, I didn't see it."

Harvey Penny, as told to David Rivers, location unspecified, January 1970. Courtesy of Folklife Archives at Kentucky Library, Western Kentucky University

Husband Returns to Bother Wife

Christian County

When we lived on Third Street in Hopkinsville, we had a ghost. It was a headless man. Me and Wayne and Maurice could see him all the time, and we used to talk to him. Mama and others thought we was crazy.

He used to just come and stand around, but the only person he bothered was his wife. Whenever she came to our house, or by our house, she would get hurt. He didn't want her there because she was going out with other men after he died.

He didn't bother us though. Daddy saw him one time when the ghost was chasing him around the house. When Daddy first saw him, he thought it was somebody else, but it was that man's ghost.

Randall Wiley, as told to Mary J. Oldham, Hopkinsville, 1972. Courtesy of Folklife Archives at Kentucky Library, Western Kentucky University

Headless Annie

Harlan County

It has been told for many years about a girl with no head wandering around on Big Black Mountain. One legend has it that there was a big dispute between some miners one night. The miners came after Annie, her father, and her mother, in order to make an example of what they would do to those who were against them.

First, they took her daddy and made Annie and her mother watch as they cut off his head and hung him up by his fat, like a pig slaughtered. Then, Annie had to watch as they raped and murdered her mother. Finally, they took this poor child and did the same thing to her.

They say if you're on Big Black Mountain at dark, about the same time she died, you can see Annie walking down looking for her head.

Brian Boggs, Cumberland, March 26, 2008

Buckets of Water Carried by Ghost

Harlan County

In a southeastern county in Kentucky, my grandmother, whom I will refer to as Sandy, had a paranormal experience. She was about nine years old at the time this incident happened. She and two of her brothers witnessed what happened. She came from a large family of thirteen children; she was the twelfth child born, so her parents were up there in age. All the children had chores that they had to do, and one of the chores she and her two brothers had to do was to go to a nearby well, about a mile and a half each way, and draw three buckets of water. All the children had done this chore before, with no incident or encounter. They had all heard stories of the headless woman drawing water from the well, but none of them had actually encountered her.

During this one trip, when they went to draw water from the well, my grandmother and her two brothers were playing, swinging their buckets around, when something caught their attention. They all looked and saw a woman carrying two buckets of water, then they called out to the woman offering to help her carry her buckets of water. The woman didn't answer, and kept walking.

They walked faster trying to catch up to the woman as they were calling out asking her if she needed help. When they got close enough, they quit calling out to her because they saw she didn't have a head.

Needless to say, they didn't get any water and ran all the way back home. But they didn't think about getting into trouble for not getting the water. When they got home, they told their parents what they had seen. Her parents had heard of the story, and my great-grandfather, from what I have been told, did not believe in such foolishness. He always said, "The dead can't hurt you; they are already dead."

He made my grandmother and her two brothers go back to the well, find their buckets, get the water, and bring it back home. They did what they were told to do, so they went back to the well and got the water. By the time they ran back home, for the second time, their buckets were only half full.

They were very watchful from then on. Every time they had to go back to that well to draw water, they always had their eyes open, and they didn't play around while they were there.

DeAnna Perkins, Cumberland, March 12, 2008

Walking Headless Ghost

Harlan County

A woman and her husband from the Big Laurel area were driving home late one night. They were very near the Pine Mountain Settlement School when the woman saw a figure up ahead. It was not unusual to see a pedestrian walking in this area, but there was something curious about this one.

As they approached, the woman noticed that the person had on overalls and a crisp white button-down shirt. That was not unusual, but what was very unusual was that this man did not have a head! The headless man turned to the car as it approached, and both the driver and passenger got a good look at him. He never disappeared.

The man and woman said they continued driving very fast and as they hurried to the safety of their home, the woman turned around and saw the headless man turn and continue to walk toward the Settlement School.

They never figured out who or what it was.

The Boggs family, as told to Darla Jackson, Big Laurel, 1981

Headless Ghost in Big White House

Rowan County

My great-grandfather and four other men went to look for work in Virginia. They came to a new house that was being built and asked if they could stay all night. The man said they didn't have room for them there, but they could go down to that big white house that he had moved out of.

They ate supper at his house and he told them the other house was haunted, but they could stay there if they wanted to. They went to that other house. There were two beds in it, and three of the men got in one bed, and the other two got in the other.

They heard something upstairs making a noise, and then somebody came walking down the stairs. Then they saw this man with no head and he walked up and down between their beds. As he walked, they could hear teeth gritting.

They left and did not stay there all night.

Jatondo Smith, as told to Bessie Sallee Marshall, Emerson, 1960.
Leonard Roberts Collection, Southern Appalachian Archives,
Berea College

Headless Murdered Man

Pike County

Marion Miller, Albert Pugh, and Jim Reed, young men in 1913, went to Freeburn, Kentucky, peddling garden produce. About dusk dark one evening they sold out and started back to Peter Creek to stay all night with a very respectable family. (The people were mean in that section at that time.)

As they were driving the wagon team up the creek, Albert saw something standing, leaning against a tree beside the road. He punched Marion, who was sitting on the seat beside him, and said, "Marion, do you see what I see? What is that?"

Marion said, "Why, that's a man with no head on him."

Albert was driving and he kept going because he was afraid to stop. As they approached the headless man, dressed in a black suit, white shirt, no tie, stepped out in front of them, about six feet in the middle of the road. Jim raised up, fainted, and fell back in the wagon. The headless man just went down into the ground in front of the wagon.

They just went on, told this family what had happened, and this family told them that a man had been murdered in that spot and buried in the middle of the road.

Several persons have seen this [ghost].

Albert Pugh, as told to Ilo Belcher, location unknown, 1971.
Leonard Roberts Collection, Southern Appalachian Archives,
Berea College

Ghost Reveals Treasure

Monroe County

It is said there was a place where nobody could stay, that people would go there to live but couldn't stay but one night until they had to leave. They'd claim that something would start from the attic and come down the stair steps like chains rattling, and you could hear somebody walking down the stair steps just as plain as you please. He then walked up to the bed and said to it, "I want to know what you want here in this house?"

It is said that sometime before that a man had been killed. Whoever killed him cut off his head while trying to get him to tell where his money was located. I suppose he'd lived in that house.

This ghost told this fellow that his head is buried in one place, but his body is in another place. The ghost then said, "If you'll go get that head and bury it with my body, I'll never bother anybody no more, and I'll also tell you where my gold is hid."

And this fellow promised to do what the ghost asked him to do, and he did it all the next day. After he got in bed, he heard the ghost coming back down the steps, with chains just rattling. It walked right up to this fellow's bed and told him that it had bored a hole in the bedpost, and because the fellow had done what it had requested, the gold in the bedpost was his. Its final words were, "The gold is yours, and I'll never bother anybody else."

As far as I know, that was all I ever heard about that ghost.

Willie Montell, Rock Bridge, 1974

Ghostly Happenings in House and Around

Rowan County

Some people don't believe in haunts and ghosts of any sort, but this story I know is true. My mother-in-law, Mrs. Lydie Stacy, moved into a house one time where a man that had killed a man lived. He said they could very often see and hear things in and around this house. It was always at night that this happened.

The house was an old log house with stairways leading up from the front bedroom. The stairway had a homemade door with just a string tied on the door, and then wrapped around a nail on the door-facing to fasten it.

About one night a week at a certain time, that string would unwind of its own accord and the stairs door would come open, and a small light would dance around on the ceiling.

Their barn was up the hollow about three hundred yards from the house. One time one of the grown boys had neglected to do the milking until it was late. He went to the barn and after he had finished his work, he started to the house and then looked up. Standing by the side of the road was a woman with no head.

Another time, Mrs. Stacy was expecting one of her married sons and his family, who lived in Lewis County. They usually came in a wagon. Her children that were home had gone to church, and when bedtime came she went to bed. In a short time, she heard a wagon roll up into the yard and then heard a voice holler at the horses. She waited, but no one ever came in. She thought maybe after seeing no light, they had gone to church.

When the children did come home from church, she was expecting her married son and family, but they did not come.

Iva Stacy, location unspecified, 1961. Leonard Roberts Collection,
Southern Appalachian Archives, Berea College

Spirit Seeks Lost Head

Ohio County

Tales of headless ghosts searching for their heads are favorite yarns. One of the best comes from Ohio County.

Around 1910 in the Sand Hill locality, near Rosine, the headless naked body of a man was discovered in a horse-drawn carriage. Not a single person who viewed the horrible spectacle would shed any light on the identity of the man or the horses and buggy. Local officials investigated, but since all attempts at identification proved fruitless, the body was turned over to the county and given a pauper's burial. Needless to say, his murderer or murderers were never apprehended. Shortly thereafter, persons passing through the area began to report strange things happening to them.

One said that he almost suffocated for lack of air. Something seemed to be taking his very breath, so he said.

Another said he felt a stream of warm air circling his neck like a rope and getting tighter and tighter until he could hardly breathe. Still others claim to have been forcibly held momentarily on the spot by some strange power which they could not see or hear.

All of them seemed to believe it was the unfortunate carriage driver's spirit seeking his lost head.

A few years later, while plowing in a field not far from the fatal spot, a farmer unearthed a human skull. Although it was commonly thought that the skull belonged to the murdered man, it was never proven.

And since no efforts were made to get the two together, residents say his spirit still haunts Sand Hill.

Frankie Hager, as told to Jim Clark, Owensboro, 1969. Courtesy of Folklife Archives at Kentucky Library, Western Kentucky University

Headless Woman

Metcalfe County

There is a place about five miles from Edmonton on the road to Curtis, a community that once had a post office. Things have been seen by different people there on a spot known as Ball Hills. Here the road passes through the woods, with a very deep woods to the east. This road runs through the woods for about a mile and a half. Near the road is a spring, and upon the hill above this spring had been a house which has long since disappeared.

The story ran that a headless woman had been seen to cross the road from this opening, and go into the woods toward the spring. Once this creature was so bold it scared a woman's horse, which threw her.

At the end of this [section of the] woods ran a creek where upon a high hilltop there stands a brick house. The old lady who lived there when I was a child kept very choice sweet potatoes for seed, and my grandfather always bought from her.

I usually went for the potatoes or plants that were needed at home. It was a terrible thing to pass and expect to see this headless woman run across the road. The fear was to me as if she had crossed [the road]. However, I never did see her.

Today this woodland has all been cleared. Two farmhouses are now on this tract. A road is being built over the spot where the ghost used to be seen. The spring to which she always went now furnishes water for the road builders.

Metcalfe County W. P. A. Report, 1936,
provided by Kay Harbison, Summer Shade

The Haint on Kendall Hill

Morgan County

There's a hill near Wrigley in Morgan County called Kendall Hill that is hainted. A number of people claim they have seen haints and strange things when they'd come across there on a dark night.

One night, Old Uncle Marion Whitt was a-coming across there and he saw a haint. He got to Wrigley as fast as he could and came to our house and told us about it. He said it was a headless man just a-standing there by the road. Everyone tried to convince him that maybe it wasn't a haint. But he'd say, "It was a haint alright. It didn't have any head, all hunched up there standing in the snow." Finally, he agreed to go back up there the next day, and since there was a big snow on, he said if there were tracks in the snow he'd know it was just a man trying to scare him. But if there weren't, he'd know it was a haint.

He tracked himself back up the hill to where he saw it. There were no tracks but his own, so he knew for sure it was the Kendall Hill Haint he'd seen.

Another time when he was coming across there on a dark night, something that looked like a headless man jumped on his horse behind him, and the horse nearly tore the road up running to Wrigley. Just before they got into the village, the haint just disappeared. Uncle Marion said it nearly squeezed him to death while it was riding with him.

Bonnie R. Lewis, location unspecified, 1959. Leonard Roberts Collection,
Southern Appalachian Archives, Berea College

Pretty Good Race

Metcalfe County

I heard about this fellow that was seen walking around in the cemetery, and he didn't have a head. He had no head whatsoever, just his shoulders down to his feet. He would walk and he would talk.

This local fellow didn't believe what he had heard about the headless man, so he went to the cemetery just to see if he could see him. When he got there, he sat down.

The fellow with no head walked up, and when he was seen by the man sitting there, it must have scared him so much that he jumped up and started running down this old path. Well, the headless man took out after him and chased him until he was about out of breath, but he still thought he was quite a bit ahead of the headless thing.

Being out of breath, he set down on a log. As soon as he did that, the headless man ran right up and set down beside him, then said, "Well, we had a pretty good race didn't we?"

Still out of breath, the man said, "Yes, we did, and we're going to have another one!"

Kay Harbison, as told by both Clayton Barnett and G. H. Harbison,
Summer Shade, September 3, 1968

Veteran's Skull

Cumberland County

My baby sister's father knew this guy that had a friend who lived in this old house. When he went there, he went inside and his friend disappeared in the darkness. Then the candles suddenly went out, but he lit one and went down the stairway. When he got down the steps, his candle flickered off and on, off and on, for something like ten times.

When he finally got it lit up again, he found himself face to face with an army guy's skull. What happened to his friend was never known.

J. Mayfield, as told to Samantha Mayfield, Burkesville,
November 1, 2007

Money Finally Found

Jefferson County

There was a big house on a big hill. Long years ago, people didn't take money to the bank. When people died, there was a chance somebody might find it. This particular family buried their money in the chimney, but all family members died out. People went to that house to find the money, and every time they would go, they heard something.

They would also see a man without a head who would disappear into the chimney. He had red eyes, and people couldn't get near him because he was so hot.

Anthony Blevins and a friend went to look for the money. They heard something in the chimney, then decided to dig. Doing this, they hit the thing that the money was in, but then a windstorm came and the money started sinking until they couldn't hold on any longer.

The grandson of Mr. Blevins's friend came back and finally found the money. The spirits then left the house.

Susie Peebles, as told to Beverly Butler, Louisville, 1972.
Courtesy of Folklife Archives at Kentucky Library,
Western Kentucky University

7

Animal Ghosts and Animal Tales

~

Ghosts That Were Not Ghosts

Hopkins County

As a child, about sixty-five years ago, we visited my grandparents often. And when we went to see them, always at night some people always came there [to visit]. They would tell all kinds of stories, and one of the ghost stories I will always remember was about sounds and other things.

Out in the county, houses were fairly close to one another. So the young men always walked to see their girlfriends along a three- or four-mile road. On this road was an old house back off of the road. It was run-down. The windows were broke, and the doors were not closed.

Well, one night this young man was walking by that old house when he heard sounds like someone walking around and up and down the stairs. He looked around and saw white shadows in the door and on the porch. He even saw white shadows in a window. These white things were everywhere! This young man ran all the way home, woke up his father, and told him what he had seen.

The father told him to be still, that they would get some men to go with them the next night to see what it was he had seen. So they did. They hid in the bushes, then about 11:00 P.M. some white things came around in the house. They heard footsteps also. They didn't know what to think, but to their surprise these white things that had always been seen and heard by many [local people] were nothing more than white goats!

They had a good time laughing.

Evelyn Joines, location unspecified, February 14, 1992.
Courtesy of Folklife Archives at Kentucky Library,
John Morgan Collection, Western Kentucky University

Disappearing Dog Ghost

Adair County

Our old family doctor, Dr. Simmons, rode a horse all the time when going to see his patients. He always said that as he passed a cemetery at Highpoint, a little white dog would run out and follow him along the highway for a short distance, then just disappear. This dog would do that during the day, or at nighttime.

He said he didn't pay much mind to it when it first started happening, but it just kept on and on. It would come out and run along after his horse, then just disappear in midair right in front of his eyes.

James Keltner, as told to Glenn E. Groebli, Columbia, 1971.
Courtesy of Folklife Archives at Kentucky Library,
Western Kentucky University

Ghostly White Fox

Larue County

This story was used by my grandmother to scare her children into going to bed, or keeping them there after they had been told to go to bed. The story goes like this:

One day my grandfather was out hunting and came upon a solid white fox. He shot at it but missed many times, but couldn't believe it because he was shooting right at it. After a few days, he saw it right behind the house and killed it, the reason being that it was a threat to the chickens and other farm animals. After he killed it, he knew it would be gone and the other animals would be alright.

A few days after the death of the fox, a cow had been killed by some sort of wild animal resembling a fox. That was the first clue to the ghost of the white fox. The second was when my grandmother got up one night to get a drink, she saw the fox run through the living room and into the kitchen. This moved her very much, so she hustled back to the bedroom to tell what had happened.

That happened a couple of other times, but only after the hour of midnight. So this was used to keep the children to bed, but she saw it one night herself.

Even when I stay with my grandmother, I will not get out of bed after midnight.

Mrs. W. E. Reed, as told to Bev Vance, Hodgenville, 1970.
Courtesy of Folklife Archives at Kentucky Library,
Western Kentucky University

Reincarnated as an Eagle

Logan County

This guy was in the service, and he was always kind and generous, but his wife was mean and selfish. And so before he died, he saw this guy who'd made him believe in reincarnation. And he knew this doctor, and from him he got this serum for reincarnation.

This serviceman always liked eagles, so he told his doctor that he wanted to be reincarnated as one. When he died, the doctor was contacted, and he gave the dead man the shot of serum. So, the man was buried in one of those house-looking things in the cemetery.

At Halloween the next year, his [widow] didn't want to give any candy to the kids. He'd left her some money to give to charities in his will, but she hadn't done it. So on Halloween, she was going to leave for the country so she wouldn't have to give out any candy. Well, she kept hearing wings flapping when she watered her garden, but when she turned around nothing was there. Also, someone else noticed that the door to his tomb was opened. Well, she started going faster in her car, and she tried to put on the brakes but that didn't help. The car ran off the road up in the air, and she looked out and saw the shadow of these huge wings, then started screaming.

All of a sudden, the car was thrown down, then the eagle scratched her face, clawed her, and left three scars on each side of her face.

I really know a lady that has three scars on both sides of her face.

Mary Ann Emberger, as told to Mary Kirk DeShazer, Russellville,
January 2, 1970. Courtesy of Folklife Archives at
Kentucky Library, Western Kentucky University

Not a Ghost, but a Rat

Logan County

Here is a story in connection with a place on the Nashville Road. A man that once owned a store was murdered in it one night. The place was then sold, and after that, several families lived in it, and all of them said it was haunted. They heard noises that sounded like a man walking up and down the steps. Finally, the family that lived in it before my uncle bought the place closed off the stairway with a door.

Uncle Snow bought the place but was never scared [of what they called Old Scratch]. He didn't believe that story at all, but one night he heard this sound like a man going down the steps. Well, Uncle Snow got a poker and stationed himself near the bottom of the steps the next night, and he killed the ghost.

It turned out to be a rat that had had its tail cut off in a trap, and when it moved this stump of a tail sounded like a person walking down the steps.

Mrs. Edward Coffman, as told to Mary Kirk DeShazer, Russellville, January 2, 1970. Courtesy of Folklife Archives at Kentucky Library, Western Kentucky University

A Panther, Not a Ghost

Logan County

There was a panther in Logan County a hundred years ago, and no one knew where it came from. A man riding home on a horse was frightened by it. My father and another man heard the panther scream, and dogs begged to be let inside the house.

Some boys out hunting heard it, and found that their dogs had treed this panther. It was a huge beast, from all accounts telling about it. One boy from town killed it and brought it into town on a horse. The panther was so large that its tail dragged along the ground.

They put it in front of one of the stores in town. That was just after slave times, and Uncle Will Clark had an old [black man]. Anyway, the old [black] man was a free man and was out hunting when he got lost. He thought if he called, someone would answer. He said, "Hooeee," and kept being answered from across the creek. It turned out to be the panther answering him.

This old man said that when he saw it was a panther, he just flew. He always said that the legs would always take care of the body.

Mrs. Edward Coffman, as told to Mary Kirk DeShazer, Russellville, January 2, 1970. Courtesy of Folklife Archives at Kentucky Library, Western Kentucky University

Ghostly Dog

Harlan County

My father tells this story about when he was younger. One night when he was coming home from church, he was riding a mule. He came across a hound that looked real pale. Well, the hound was staying just right in front of him in the road, and he wasn't going to go around it.

The next thing he knew, that hound was on the other side of him, and it hadn't gone between the mule's legs. But the mule was half scared to death of the hound, but my father was determined to go back and run over the dog ghost. When he did that, the same thing happened. The hound went right through his mule.

Edna Howard, as told to Bob Blanton, Loyall, November 1, 1970. Courtesy of Folklife Archives at Kentucky Library, Western Kentucky University

The Ghost Rock

Boyd County

There's a place near here that was, and still is, called "The Ghost Rock."

Some people say they have seen men there with no heads. One cold, cold night I was passing by there and heard chains rattling. I got about half scared, so I went on up to the house.

My mother and sister were already in bed, so I got my shotgun and went back to the rock. I was riding a four-year-old mare, and she was as wild as a Red River bull! Well, I laid the bridle reins down on the brush, then went to find out what I had heard. I got up there and I heard rattling. I looked around and the moon was shining, but it was a little cloudy. My brother had set a steel trap there and had caught a rabbit.

I went back home and he was in the bed. I woke him up and told him that I had found out what the ghost was. I said it was a rabbit in that steel trap he had set. He then said, "Well, believe it or not, I set that trap last season."

Thomas Compton, as told to Dennis Reller, Boyd County, 1972.
Courtesy of Folklife Archives at Kentucky Library,
Western Kentucky University

Mouse Tries to Escape

Jefferson County

One night my mother and dad had gone to bed, and they heard a noise. They didn't know where in the world it was coming from. My daddy told my mother that they'd better get up to see what it was, and if she would carry the lantern, he would take the poker from the stove, and they would try to find out what was making that noise.

They went outside the house, and were walking around to see what they might find. They looked in all the chicken coops, the smokehouse, and they didn't find a thing, so they came back in the house, put out the lantern, then went back to bed.

They heard the same noise again. So this time, they went upstairs to look around. They heard something in a stone jar, and they looked in it. It was a little mouse jumping up and down, and that's what all that noise was about.

Walter Wimsatt Sr., as told to Donna Sue Smith, Louisville,
November 11, 1972. Courtesy of Folklife Archives at
Kentucky Library, Western Kentucky University

Thought to Be a Ghost

Jefferson County

This man had been out all day, and was coming home that night through the woods. He had taken a shot of white lightening. He was riding a horse, and it was midnight, or one o'clock in the morning.

Suddenly, he saw a [white] light come through the trees, and when he saw it, it looked like it was going from the ground up to the sky. It kept going and coming up and down. He hollered out, but no one answered. He hollered again, still no one answered. So he pulled out his pistol and shot it. When he did this, an old cow jumped up and went "Moo, Moo, Moo," as she ran across the field.

Walter Wimsatt Sr., as told to Donna Sue Smith, Louisville, November 11, 1972. Courtesy of Folklife Archives at Kentucky Library, Western Kentucky University

The Cat in the Coffin

Floyd County

Back in the days of my great-grandparents, I don't know what year, there was a family that they had heard about, and this is the story as it was told to them.

This family lived in the Floyd County area. One of the family members had passed away, so they did the usual thing we normally do. They had the dead person's body somewhere so family and friends could come and pay their respects. They had a funeral service in church, then kept them three days and mourned their loss.

The day finally came to bury the body, so they all went to the cemetery for the graveside ceremony. As accustomed, they were going to have church on the cemetery and let everyone pass by to say their last good-byes.

Well, when the undertaker opened up the coffin, a big black cat jumped out. They could never figure out where the cat came from, or how it got into the coffin, because someone had been there the whole time, and when they closed the lid on the coffin to take it to the cemetery, there wasn't a cat in it. It really startled the people, and nothing was ever found out about where the cat came from.

I guess it will always be a mystery.

Yvonetta Prater, Big Sandy Community and Technical College, February 2008

The Barn Ghost

Jefferson County

This entire community knew of the ghost in the old log barn. No one could explain the reason for the ghost being there, but everyone knew he was there. The ghost played among the rafters and hay loft about every night. Many had seen the ghost and even more had heard it drag a chain along the board floors. The livestock refused to go into the barn at night. Occasionally, in the stillness of the night, screams could be heard coming from the barn.

The old barn was a landmark in the community. It had stood for several generations on the old Beck farm. The barn was still used regularly, but the boys always managed to get the chores done early enough in the evening to get out of the barn before it got dark.

Mr. Beck thought he had seen the ghost early one morning. He always got up long before daybreak and by the time it was light enough to see, he always had the stock fed. One morning he let the horses into the barn lot and he went up to the loft to throw down some hay for the horses to eat. He had always told the boys to place the pitchfork close to the barn beam near the ladder. Jerry Beck had some reason to go into the loft the night before, and in his haste to get out of the barn he dropped the pitchfork on the hay. The next morning when Mr. Beck went out into the barn, he had to feel around for the pitchfork before he could feed the stock.

While he was searching for the pitchfork, he touched something warm and soft. He drew back quickly and the next moment his other hand fell across a man's foot. Mr. Beck let out a yell loud enough that it was heard by the neighbors a half mile away. The ghost turned out to be a tramp who was using the hayloft as a bed.

Jerry knew he had walked into the ghost early one morning as he went around the corner of the old barn on his way to the pasture to get the cows. As he stepped around the corner, something big and white came right up out of the ground and waved its white arms in the air, but it didn't make any noise. Jerry didn't take a second look. He headed toward the house as fast as his legs would travel. He was running and yelling at the same time.

After he calmed down and told his father what happened, his dad decided he was going to get his shotgun and go to the barn and get rid of the ghost. When Mr. Beck came back to the house, he said Jerry's ghost was a little white calf that had been lying along beside of the barn. As Jerry came around the corner of the barn, the calf had gotten to its feet and was switching its tail, which looked like a ghost coming out of the ground waving its white arms.

In spite of all these discoveries, everyone knew that the old barn was haunted. Jerry came home one night from a dance and, as usual, he rode his horse into the lot and jerked his saddle off and threw it on the ground and turned his horse loose. He wouldn't hang his saddle up, or put his horse in the stable on the rainiest night.

On this particular night, Jerry had drank a little too much at the dance, but his brain was not messed up enough to keep him from thinking of a ghost as he rode into the lot. He had ridden his horse into the lot under the old elm tree and was in the act of removing the saddle when "clank, clank, clank," began the ghost's chain rattling across the barn floor. "Thump, thump, thump," the steady walk of something could be heard. Jerry's hair seemed to stand on end. All at once he became sober and he threw his saddle and bridle on the ground.

He ran toward the house and jumped the gate. After he was over the gate, he stopped and looked toward the barn. The lower half of the barn door was closed and there dancing about on the upper half of the door was the ghost. The ghost was dancing from one side to the other in the door.

Jerry looked no more. He ran to the house and woke his father up. He told his dad that the ghost was in the barn again. Mr. Beck got out of bed and got his gun. They ran out of the house toward the barn. As they neared the barn, they slowed down a little, then stopped when they got to the gate. Mr. Beck raised his gun and aimed it at the ghost, but when he was about to squeeze the trigger, Jerry yelled, "Stop, stop." Old Charlie, the bald-faced horse had opened the barn door and was inside the barn.

The lower barn door had blown shut and fastened, and the old horse was looking out over the door with only his white nose and forehead showing through the darkness, giving the appearance of a dancing ghost as he moved his head from side to side. His chain halter dragged across the barn floor.

That solved the mystery of the log barn ghost!

Hamilton Kessler, as told to Bobby Zachery, location unspecified, 1961.
D. K. Wilgus Collection, Southern Appalachian Archives,
Berea College

Was It a Cat Ghost?

Daviess County

I was just sixteen when I and my younger sister, Ora, first became aware of the mystery in our bedroom. Our home was out in the country between Owensboro and Stanley. It was an old house built of logs and was weatherboarded. It had a pretty yard with lilacs and roses.

There was one large room upstairs where Ora and I slept, and that is where the mystery was. When we put out the light and went to bed, we could feel something jump on the bed very lightly, like a cat, and start walking toward the head of the bed. When it got there, it just disappeared. We would try raising up the covers real quick, but there was nothing there.

We never knew what it was, but I know it was not just our imagination.

Jesse Dorris, as told to Jim L. Clark, Owensboro, April 8, 1969.
Courtesy of Folklife Archives at Kentucky Library,
Western Kentucky University

Ghost Cats in Old House

Trigg or Lyon County

I had asked Dad to tell me the story about the haunted house that Grandad and Grandmother Dycus lived in down in the "Bend of the River" shortly after they got married. Both of them had been married before. He had nine children at the time, and she had six, thus they were badly in need of a larger house. They were able to move into the house because of the strange experiences of the two families that had lived there.

Dad said, "Oh, yes. I knew the people in both families. They had this farm rented. It was a big house, a very large house for those days. It was a double house that had a big hall about twelve feet wide between the buildings. One family lived on one side of the hall and the other family lived on the other side. They cultivated this big place together.

"One night one of them saw a cat jump up into the window on his side. Pretty soon another cat jumped up. And when the cats filled up the window, he went across the hall to his partner and told him to come take a look. So they came in there and he saw the cats in the window. So they both went to the door at the end of the hallway. They opened up the door and saw that the yard was full of cats. So they stepped out of the hall door, and one of them went one way, and one the other way, driving the cats in front of them. I don't know if they were crowded to start with, or how they managed to drive the cats along, unless they were flying all over. . . . So when they got around the house and met at the other end of the hall, the cats were all gone. Well, they stayed there the rest of that night, but the next day they both moved out. They said they would not stay there any more. . . .

"So the crop was laid by, but it wasn't matured yet. Mother and Dad hadn't been married very long, and they were putting their two families together. They needed a lot more room than there was in the place Dad lived. So they went to see about that, and Dad rented the farm from which these two fellows had left. Dad also bought their corn crop right in the field, and he had to take his chances on the corn maturing without getting frostbit, or bit up by the wind, or what have you. He would have to harvest the corn in the fall. He got their crop for a very reasonable cost, but he gave a promissory note for it since he didn't have enough money to pay for it."

When I found this promissory note among my father's papers, it confirmed the facts of this story.

Catherine Dycus, as told by her father, Hampton, Virginia, February 15, 1992. Courtesy of Folklife Archives at Kentucky Library, John Morgan Collection, Western Kentucky University

Strange Fire Ball and Dog in the House

Hopkins County

Many communities have haunted houses. In the Beulah neighborhood, the house was about one mile from any other dwelling. There were old graves around the Lynn House. People said that travelers that stopped there for the night were killed, robbed, and buried in the backyard. These activities took place at least 150 years ago.

Sixty years ago, Sally and Edd Hicks married and set up house-keeping there. Sally, who still lives and is considered a truthful woman, was not easily frightened, but Edd could easily be frightened. Not long ago, Sally said to me that she didn't like to tell about her experiences since people laughed at her. She said that perhaps we didn't have some things now that we did have back then. She told me earnestly that there were queer things that went on at that house.

One night, Sally awoke to see a great ball of fire in the corner of her room. She got up to extinguish it, but it wasn't there. The next time she saw it, she covered up her head until it was gone.

Later on, a large dog reared up on her bed one night. It was a strange dog and twice as large as any dog she had ever seen. Sally and Edd moved the next day, and the house was never occupied after that.

Mrs. Lewis Good, location unspecified, 1950. D. K. Wilgus Collection, Southern Appalachian Archives, Berea College

The Three Cats

Martin County

There once was an old preacher who moved into a new community as pastor of the local church. He had arrived earlier than expected, and his congregation didn't as yet have a place for him to stay. When he got in town they somehow told of their embarrassing predicament, and the old preacher didn't in the least seem to be alarmed. He said he would be glad to stay anywhere, for as he put it, God's chosen ones ain't choosy.

After somewhat of a frenzied search with little luck, they found an old house for the preacher to stay in. He again said he didn't mind, and when they told him it was supposed to be haunted, he just laughed at them and assured them that no man of God was afraid of ghosts or anything supernatural.

He gladly moved into the large two-story house, it being all dirty and somewhat spooky, he thought. The preacher didn't mind much though, for as soon as it got dark, he built a good fire in the fireplace and sat down to read his Bible by the firelight.

Soon after he settled down for a good reading, an average size cat walked into the front room past the preacher and sat down next to the fire, then promptly spit into the fire and rubbed its front paws together. The preacher never thought much about this as he was always around cats and knew to expect anything from the furry creatures.

Just as he sat down to begin reading again, another cat walked into the room, only this time the cat was much larger, much the same size as a goodly sized dog. It, too, sat down in front of the fire, spit into the red flame, and rubbed its paws together, much as one would while warming before a warm flame after cold weather.

The preacher never thought much about it, but did think it odd that two cats would sit side by side near the fire, especially when one was twice as big as the other. But remembering the Christian upbringing he had had, he began to read again and think nothing about it.

Eventually, a third cat walked into the room, only this one was closer to the size of a lion than a cat, but it did look just like a cat. It also sat down next to the fire with his buddies and spit into the deep warm flame and rubbed his hands together. This time the preacher thought he rubbed his hands together like he might be ready for a big meal. He was sure getting scared now.

Finally, the smallest of the three cats looked over at the big one and asked, "When do we begin?"

He was promptly answered by the biggest one that said, "As soon as big Mo gets here."

The preacher ran out of the house, leaving his Bible and was never seen or heard of again.

Mrs. Opal Marcum, as told to Homer Marcum, Lovely, 1969.
Leonard Roberts Collection, Southern Appalachian Archives,
Berea College

The Fox Face Girl

Harlan County

My mom always told us the story about a young girl walking through the woods. She said it was getting late in the evening, right at the edge of dark. And as she was walking, a fox bit her on the leg, causing her to have to limp on the way home.

For several days after that, she ran a high fever. Everyone that saw her said that her face turned into the shape of a fox. The only time she would leave the house was at night.

After several weeks, no one saw the Fox Face Girl again.

Teresa Boggs, Cumberland, March 26, 2008

8

GHOSTLY LIGHTS AND SCREAMS

~

Fisher Ridge Light

Hart County

There is a community in Hart County known as Fisher Ridge. Back in the 1930s and 1940s there was a man that lived on a farm that had several acres in it. His name is John Bishop, and he is now deceased. He was a big man and ruled over his family with a strong hand. He ran his boys off from home as they reached their teen years. His wife never left the farm. I don't remember ever seeing her. He claimed not to believe in anything, neither heaven or hell.

Among his valuables was a prize pair of foxhounds. People came from far and near trying to buy them, but he wouldn't sell them for any price. The story goes that many neighbors and friends came to go hunting with him, bringing their young hounds along to be trained by Mr. Bishop's famous dogs. His older sons went hunting with him a lot, also. But every night, when they came to a certain ridge on the farm, a light would appear in front of them, about as high as an average man's head. It would move slowly and stop every few feet as if it wanted them to follow it.

This made Mr. Bishop very mad because once this light appeared, the hounds came whining and cuddled at the men's feet. No amount of trying to get them to leave would get them to leave the side of their master. So when the light appeared, they all knew the fox hunt was over. Many times, Mr. Bishop wanted to follow the light, but his sons and friends raised such a fuss that he always gave in and went back to the house with them.

One rainy, damp Sunday night, his boys were gone. And no neighbors came around to go hunting. Mr. Bishop put on his coat and boots and told his wife he was going to take his hounds out for awhile. Getting his gun, he went on his way.

His wife waited up for him until midnight, then finally fell asleep. At 3:00 A.M., Mr. Bishop came wandering in. He was as pale as a ghost and looked as if he was walking in a daze. He was wet, as if he had fallen into the river, and was shaking with chills. He looked at his wife with eyes that looked like he was just staring into space and wouldn't answer when she talked to him. She got him undressed and into bed, then spooned a few bites of hot soup into him. For three days he never moved from that bed, except to go to the bathroom. He never ate, never said a bad word to anyone. Finally, on the fourth day he got up and dressed, then got his horses hooked to the wagon and took that prized pair of foxhounds to Horse Cave and sold them to a guy who had been wanting to buy them for a long time.

Never again did Mr. Bishop go hunting, and he would never let his sons or neighbors go hunting on his farm again. Time passed, and Mr. Bishop and his wife died. The farm was sold to three brothers who also had foxhounds, and fox hunted on the farm. The farm has changed, but never again did anyone ever mention seeing the Fisher Ridge light.

This story was told to me by my grandfather, who heard it from one of the older Bishop boys, who said he'd been with his father when they saw the light. Later, when I was a teenager, the same story was told to me by the youngest Bishop boy, who had been too young to go on the fox hunts, but said his mother had told the story to him.

Geraldine Norman, location unspecified, March 1992.
Courtesy of Folklife Archives at Kentucky Library,
John Morgan Collection, Western Kentucky University

Lights in Graveyard

Monroe County

There's an old graveyard down here in the field by Barney Parrish's where lights have been seen. I don't know whether there's any Indians buried there or not. But it's an old, old graveyard. Lights have been seen there, and we've even seen them ourselves. I've seen streaks of fire dart right in front of me, just great big streaks.

Elsworth Carter, as told to his nephew, Rock Bridge, 1974

Candle Seen on Casket

Graves County

There was an old woman that lived in a red brick house that wasn't furnished with electricity, so she had to light up her house with red candles.

One day she died, so they put her casket on a table in front of a window with a candle on top of the casket. It is said that if you pass by her house at midnight, you can see a candle burning in the window.

Joe Deaton, as told to William Deaton, location unspecified, 1972. Courtesy of Folklife Archives at Kentucky Library, Western Kentucky University

Soldier's Ghostly Screams

Fayette County

There is a big house just south of Lexington on Highway 27. Years ago, a mother was standing in front of a window in the front bedroom of the house and saw her son get off the bus. He was home on leave from the army.

Just as he stepped off the bus, a car came into the curve and killed him. The mother slammed the shutters closed, and they stayed closed even to this day, because when you open them you can hear the screams of the young man. I have passed this house hundreds of times and have never seen these shutters open, even though all the other shutters in the house are open.

Janice Simmons, Glasgow, December 1972. Courtesy of Folklife Archives at Kentucky Library, Western Kentucky University

The Screaming Skull

Butler County

This is a story that has been told and retold in Butler County about "Skull Bone Cave," or "The Screaming Skull." According to the story, many, many, many years ago a woman and her child were murdered in their home by Indians in Grayson County. When the man discovered their deaths and believed an Indian was responsible for this, he set out for revenge.

Going to an Indian camp, he saw only one person there, and thinking he was the one who had murdered his wife and child, he fired a shot and killed him. Not wanting to leave the body there, he took it to an old cave and buried it in a shallow grave in northern Butler County. This was either in the community of Grancer or Decker, depending on the story being told, but it is agreed that it is in Butler County.

The years went by and Mason Embry came to Butler County in the early 1800s, and on the property he bought and settled on was the cave where the body was buried. After hearing about the murder of the woman and child and the revenge taken, he started looking for the grave. He did indeed find parts of a skeleton in the cave, and wanting to show others, he removed the skull and took it home with him.

It has even been said that he used it at times to cover corn when gardening, using it as a hoe-type instrument. Whatever he did with the skull, it soon came back to haunt him. He began hearing terrifying screams that relentlessly followed him. He became convinced that the screams were the result of removing the skull he found in the cave, so he took it back and reburied it.

The screams were finally silenced but certainly never forgotten, as this story has lived all these years and has been locally known as "the screaming skull."

Connie Embry, Roundhill community, December 16, 2007

Old Doc Milligan

Butler County

My good friend told me this story about a house where she grew up, and where her father still lives. This place is located in the Roundhill community, Butler County, and is referred to as "Milligan Holler" by the locals. She said in former years this house had belonged to a doctor known as Old Doc Milligan. He had his practice in the house and saw his patients in what was the kitchen in my friend's time.

She said there were old glass transoms over the doors, and when she was growing up it was nothing to see a glow coming through the transom over the door that had been Old Doc Milligan's exam room when no light was on. Things were disappearing and reappearing, and keeping a screen door latched was almost impossible.

My friend said that one tale that had been told in the community was about a family that had been traveling through the area by horse and buggy when their young daughter fell ill. They heard about Old Doc Milligan and decided to stop at his place to see if he could be of any help to their teenage daughter. The doctor's treatments did not prove effective, so the young girl passed away.

The family had to move on, and the old doctor asked if he could keep the body to see if he could determine what had caused the illness that took their daughter's life. The parents agreed and the doctor studied the girl, but if a cause were discovered it wasn't handed down in the telling of this story. What was handed down was that area residents said when the wind blew you could hear a rattling sound, and they believed it was the bones of the young girl that was left at the old Doc Milligan's house.

Connie Embry, Roundhill community, December 16, 2007

Son's Screams and Scratches

Fayette County

One time in the early 1900s there was a very prominent family outside of Lexington that had a very promiscuous son that no one could handle. As the years went by, the son was the center of much turmoil that was caused in the surrounding area. The parents were scared of him because they could in no way control his actions. He was just considered impossible to do anything with.

One day the no-good son was bothering his younger brother when the brother hit him with a rock and knocked him out. The brother was scared because he thought he had killed his brother.

In this family's cellar was a huge walk-in freezer in which they kept their beef and vegetables, and no one went down there except once a week for the week's needed food. The boy remembered this and dragged his brother down the steps and locked him in the freezer.

The parents began missing the son, so they formed a search party that lasted for three days until one day the maid went down to the freezer for some food and saw a body, with bloody fingers, frozen to death. The boy had tried to escape but no one heard his cries.

The family was so shook up that they left the house and sold it to a young couple. The couple stayed for only one week before being run out by screams and scratching in the cellar during the night.

This house has been vacant ever since, and at night it is said that screams and scratching can be heard just like the sounds made by the boy.

Bev Vance, Hodgenville, 1970. Courtesy of Folklife Archives at
Kentucky Library, Western Kentucky University

Weird Noises in Old House

Daviess County

Even after we moved from the country to Owensboro in a house on Ford Avenue, we were still plagued by strange happenings. The five-room house with one room upstairs is still there on Ford Avenue off Frederica Street. The house is like the one in the country. The steps have a door at the bottom, and we could hear a sound like someone walking heavy down the steps, then stopping at the door. When we opened the door not a thing would be there. Mama and all of us heard it.

At the same house there is a cistern on the back porch, and we could hear a noise like someone pumping water. If you have ever heard one, you know how the cups clank, but when we investigated, all was as still as could be.

I guess there was an explanation for all this, but we never found one. That house was a lot like the one out in the country, and it had an old-fashioned yard with lilacs and roses. All those things that happened occurred lots of times, not just once.

Jesse Dorris, as told to Jim L. Clark, Owensboro, April 6, 1969.
Courtesy of Folklife Archives at Kentucky Library,
Western Kentucky University

Knocking Noises

Daviess County

Back in the 1800s when the living quarters for the sheriff and his deputy were located in a northwest room on the second story of the old court-house, word got around that the place was haunted. It seemed for some time that Sheriff Wilson and Deputy Jones had been annoyed at night by strange knocking sounds in the hallway outside their door.

One Sunday night, the sound awoke them as it moved for the first time through the door and over to a heavy old office desk located in the middle of the room. When they rose to investigate it, the noise ceased. But when they returned to bed, it started again.

The knocking continued for at least a year or more, and townspeople whispered that it was the ghost of Louie Angell, an old wanderer who dropped dead at the courthouse years ago in the very doorway of the room where Wilson and Jones slept.

Frankie Hager, as told to Jim L. Clark, Owensboro, April 10, 1969.
Courtesy of Folklife Archives at Kentucky Library,
Western Kentucky University

Bloodstains and Rolling Marbles

Henderson County

When I was fourteen, we moved out into the country. We had to take a small house for a few weeks until the larger one was available. This house was on the J. S. Brumley farm between the Wayne Bridge and the Lydanne Bridge over Panther Creek—rich black farmland, drained properly and tilled. We, the Garrett children, enjoyed following the ditches for hours, poking into them, jumping them, or wading. We usually went home with wet feet, a chill, and muddy clothes.

The little house we moved into was haunted, and that suited us children. A man had been murdered there many years ago, and strange noises were heard, along with seeing white articles that looked like sheets waving around at various times.

We were all intent on standing whatever we had to, for I was anxious to get back into the old Wayne School again, where all the best buddies in the world was, plus the best teachers with ability to satisfy a curious but happy little mind.

Oh, yes, I had come from the city school and had a taste of music and art, but not enough that it could be noticed in any way as far as the grades went. I was immediately placed in a higher grade in town. I was much complimented, and although I did not like much of the ways they taught, nothing could compare with Wayne School, which is still very sacred and very dear to me.

To go through living in a haunted house for a few months—the floor had a big, dark red stain of blood that was supposed to have run from the murdered man's body all the way back up under the bed. My mother really scrubbed the floor and put concentrated lye on the floor, but the stain did not come off. When we went to bed, sometimes a big marble would roll from one corner of the room to another. All night, it would roll out like that, but it stopped when the light was lit.

If the kitchen was dark, the marbles also rolled there, or if the upstairs bedroom was dark, that was where the rolling noise was located. But the light would always stop it. We moved out of the house soon, and left the bloodstain on the floor, and the rolling marble.

Sena Smithhart, as told to Jim L. Clark, Henderson,
February 21, 1969. Courtesy of Folklife Archives at
Kentucky Library, Western Kentucky University

Car That Disappeared

Barren County

My cousin Calvin Rossi was driving alone down an old marsh road. The road was real narrow and was paved with oyster shells. Suddenly, Calvin saw a light down the road, so he pulled over the first place he could, because he thought it was a car, and he knew there wasn't enough room for them to pass each other. The light stopped, too.

After waiting for what seemed like several minutes, Calvin pulled back on the road. When he got to the spot where he had seen the light, there was no car there and no place for several miles in which to turn around. He didn't stop, but drove just as fast as he dared all the way home.

I can't remember if anything strange happened after that or not. That was a long time ago.

Woodrow Simmons, as told to Janice Simmons, Glasgow,
November 1972. Courtesy of Folklife Archives at
Kentucky Library, Western Kentucky University

Horn Continues to Blow

Logan County

One time, this man ran over a little boy, and it was a hit and run. Every night after that, the man saw his car lights blinking on and off for no reason, and his horn started blowing, and all such things happened to his car.

He finally got tired of trying to fix it, because he had disconnected the horn, but it'd still be blowing. Finally, the man went crazy and died. When his neighbors found him, his face had grown years younger and he looked just like the little boy he had killed.

Kathy DeShazer, as told to Mary Kirk DeShazer, Russellville,
January 2, 1970. Courtesy of Folklife Archives at
Kentucky Library, Western Kentucky University

Weird Sounds in an Old House

Caldwell County

I don't know the name of the place along the road to Princeton, but there's a set of crooked curves as you're traveling along. I've heard that you can be traveling along there about midnight and see the lights on in this old abandoned house. If you drive up to the house and get out of the car, the lights go out and you don't see them again. What you hear sounds like people walking around in the house, and steps are squeaking. You can look in the window, but not see anything.

All you can hear are squeaks all over the place, and chains or something, rattling. I don't know what it is, but it sure is kinda spooky.

Harold Linzy, as told to Frances Gould, Crittenden County,
May 8, 1973. Courtesy of Folklife Archives at
Kentucky Library, Western Kentucky University

Cooking Chitterlings

Christian County

A lady died in the house in which we presently live. Evidently she loved chitterlings, because every time Mom cooks them mysterious things happen. When the pot is finished cooking, and just sitting on the stove cooling, the odor is not as prominent as when they are cooking.

After everyone has left the kitchen, we hear the rattling of pots, and the odor of chitterlings can be smelled. There is never anyone in the kitchen at that time, and seldom are there many people here in the house.

Mary J. Oldham, Hopkinsville, 1972. Courtesy of Folklife Archives at Kentucky Library, Western Kentucky University

Return of Dear Friend as a Ghost

Wayne County

A group of boys were working out in a gym, and one of them fell and was killed. The best friend of the dead boy was deeply upset.

There were reports about a strange light at night in the gym. The living friend thought it might be his dead friend trying to communicate with the living, so he decided to spend the night in the gym.

He was there for several hours, and the light appeared. It was indeed his friend, who told him not to worry about him any more because he was happy.

Donita Crawford, as told to Bob Blanton, Monticello, November 18, 1970. Courtesy of Folklife Archives at Kentucky Library, Western Kentucky University

Boys Frightened by Screams

Grayson County

There were two boys fishing in a creek one afternoon. After several hours of fishing, they heard a terrible scream from far down the creek. It was too far for recognition, and the boys kept fishing. Soon, they again heard the scream. It was long and finally stopped by trailing off into sobs. This time, the scream sounded even closer to them.

While the boys were thinking about leaving, they heard the scream again, this time just across the creek from them. The boys were just frozen with fright. Just then, they heard their father calling them, so they broke and ran back to the house.

Larry Elmore, as told to Bob Blanton, Leitchfield, November 2, 1970.
Courtesy of Folklife Archives at Kentucky Library,
Western Kentucky University

Ghost Hands Scratch House

Hancock County

There was a man whose wife had died, and after awhile he began to run around to play cards. One night when he was playing cards, there was a scratching sound heard. He jumped up and ran outside.

Around the house there were many lilac bushes which were the favorite flowers of the man's deceased wife. As he looked at them, he saw a hand reaching out from under one of the bushes. It was his wife's hand, and it was scratching the house.

Actually, she didn't die naturally, but was killed by her husband.

Edna Henning, as told to Bob Blanton, Lewisport, December 6, 1970.
Courtesy of Folklife Archives at Kentucky Library,
Western Kentucky University

The Haunted Bluff

Edmonson County

At night you could hear the voice of an old woman screaming, and then later you could hear voices like babies crying. Then, on dark nights, you could see big bright lights shining out from the bluff. People said they had seen something that looked like blood running off the rocks on the bluff.

I don't know what caused these voices we heard, but the next day after we heard the screaming, we would go to the bluff, but there was never anything there.

Bertha Houchin, as told to Gary Watt, Chalybeate community, 1972.
Courtesy of Folklife Archives at Kentucky Library,
Western Kentucky University

The Weird Bonnet

Edmonson County

I'll tell the story about Martha Gibson's old bonnet. She wore this old split bonnet all day long. There was a sound that would hit the top of her bonnet that sounded like a big drip of water. It would go on like this all day long. Then at night, when she'd go to bed, she'd hang her bonnet on a chair beside her bed. Then she'd tell her bonnet to go to her brothers and drip there. And sure enough, it would start dripping at the top of their bed.

They'd pull the covers up over their heads, then holler and tell their mother to make Martha set her bonnet away from them. When she heard them, she'd call it back to her bed and it would start dripping at the head of her bed.

Bertha Houchin, as told to Gary Watt, Chalybeate community, 1972.
Courtesy of Folklife Archives at Kentucky Library,
Western Kentucky University

Chopping Sounds

Lawrence County

After I was married a few years ago, we lived at the mouth of Tunnel Hollow on the left fork of Nats Creek. Since this was during the Depression years, I had to burn wood instead of coal for heat. Every night I chopped wood for the fire before supper and would leave my axe in the woodshed.

Each night, somewhere around ten o'clock, the sound of someone chopping wood would wake me up. I went out and looked several times, but no one was around. Well, one night I decided to set a trap. I rigged up the axe with a string on it so if someone bothered it, a rock would fall on a wash tub. I went into the house and went to bed and waited. Around twelve or one o'clock, the chopping started again. After several tries, I couldn't find anything out about it, and the chopping went on every night until I moved.

Now, I work as a night watchman in Tunnel Hollow. I sat in my truck several nights just below where the house was. I still hear the chopping every night I am there.

Walt Boyd, as told to Isaac Hinkle, Tadpole, November 1973. Courtesy of Folklife Archives at Kentucky Library, Western Kentucky University

Rattling Ashes

Lawrence County

During the forties, our house was heated by coal burning grates in each room. The ashes had to be rattled out of the bottom of these grates to keep them burning right.

One night Dad went to bed a little earlier than Mom, so he put a little extra coal on the fire so it would be warm when she went to bed. He dozed off after a short while, but he was awakened by someone rattling down the ashes. He naturally thought it was Mom coming to bed, so he dozed off again. Then he was awakened again by the ashes being rattled. He rolled over and no one was there. This time, he stayed awake until Mom came to bed.

When she came up, he asked her if she or anyone else in the family had been in the room since he had been asleep. She told him that everyone else was asleep and that she had just come up for the first time.

He never could figure out what that strange noise was all about.

Buddy Hinkle, as told to Isaac Hinkle, Richardson, November 1973. Courtesy of Folklife Archives at Kentucky Library, Western Kentucky University

Whimpering of a Dead Boy

Lawrence County

During the early part of her marriage, Bell Fitch and her husband, Charlie, lived on Burgess Branch of Nats Creek. Charlie's brother and his family lived close by. One day Charlie's brother and his wife had to go into town, which at that time was a two-day trip. They left their baby with Bell and Charlie, and left early in the morning.

The baby was at the age where it liked to crawl and explore. That afternoon, Charlie went hunting and left Bell and the baby there in the house alone. Bell went on about her chores after she thought she had the baby asleep on the bed. However, the child must have awakened and wandered off while Bell was outside.

Before she had finished her work, Bell heard the baby whimpering, not crying, but more like a sick babble. She went into the house to check on the baby, but couldn't find it. But she could still hear the whimpering.

After awhile, Charlie came back, and he could also hear the baby, but neither one of them could find it. They looked all that night without any luck. The whimpering didn't stop until the following morning. After it stopped, they looked that much harder, but were unable to locate the baby. However, the next day they found a bloody sock stuffed up under a rock beside the creek, about a quarter of a mile from the house. This sock was the only clue to the child that was ever found.

Buddy Hinkle, as told to Isaac Hinkle, Richardson, November 1973. Courtesy of Folklife Archives at Kentucky Library, Western Kentucky University

Screams of Husband and Wife

Lawrence County

At the point where Nats Creek runs into Big Sandy River, there is a railroad bridge that crosses Nats Creek. One night a woman was crossing the bridge on her way home when she heard a train coming. She got excited and started running, but tripped and caught her leg in between the ties. She hurt her leg and arm, so she was unable to get out.

She began to scream, and her husband, who was at the house, which was a little ways from the track, heard her. He ran down to help her, but didn't notice the train coming. When she screamed at him to get back, he didn't understand her, so the train hit them both. Pieces of their bodies were knocked into Nats Creek.

These days, every time a train passes after dark, it is said the husband and wife can still be heard screaming.

Bud Hawk Runyons, as told to Isaac Hinkle, Peach Orchard, November 1973. Courtesy of Folklife Archives at Kentucky Library, Western Kentucky University

Sounds from the Bushes

Lawrence County

When I lived on Wildcat, I worked at cutting timber in Wolfpen on Chestnut. It was about a three-mile walk through the hills from my house to the job, so I had to leave every morning before daylight. Sometimes we had to work late, and I wouldn't get home before nine or ten o'clock at night.

One night, after working late, I was walking home and heard something in the bushes. I figured it might be a snake, so I stopped to see if I could find it. Suddenly, I couldn't hear it anymore. I looked around and couldn't find anything, so I started on home, but as soon as I started walking, I heard it again. I stopped again but didn't hear nothing, so I went on.

All the way home that night, I kept hearing the noise, but I could never find out where it was coming from. It sounded like someone walking behind me, but I could never see them.

I walked that same path for a year after I heard that noise, but never heard it again.

Walt Boyd, as told to Isaac Hinkle, Tadpole, November 1973.
Courtesy of Folklife Archives at Kentucky Library,
Western Kentucky University

Preacher's Screams

Lawrence County

Several years ago, the minister of the Mt. Zion Baptist Church slipped and fell on the steps coming down from the altar and cracked his skull. He slipped and fell because a leak in the roof caused a wet spot on the steps. He died almost instantly, but he did live long enough to scream in agony, which brought several people to his aid.

Now it is said that every time it storms, you can hear him scream.

David Fitch, as told to Isaac Hinkle, Peach Orchard, November 1973.
Courtesy of Folklife Archives at Kentucky Library,
Western Kentucky University

Noisy Bones

County Unknown

The house my father was born in was in a valley. Some years before that, a man had been killed on the mountain above the house. Somehow, one of the bones of this man got lodged in the rafters of the house. One day, my grandmother got tired of having a bone above them, so my grandfather got the bone and took it down away from the house, then buried it.

That night, they heard noises that were so loud that it kept everyone in the house awake. The noise was coming in the direction of where the bone was buried. So my grandfather went down and dug up the bone, then brought it back to the house. When he got in the house with the bone, the noise stopped.

Rebecca Combs, as told to Rhonda Halgash, Louisville, December 4, 1950.
Courtesy of Folklife Archives at Kentucky Library,
Western Kentucky University

Noises in House

Russell County

When I was a young man, me and two of the men I work with were offered a chance to own ourselves a little farm for a little of nothing in terms of money. There was an old house on the farm that was supposed to be haunted, and had been ever since an old woman who once lived in it was murdered along with her three children up in the attic. The way it was told to me was that their heads were cut off.

Well, one of that old woman's kinfolk got title to the place, and since the land was better than his, he moved over to the house. The first night he moved in, some strange noises scared him off. This fellow was pretty superstitious, so he decided to rent out the house and build himself a little house.

He tried to rent the place to a couple of people, but they never managed to spend the night before noises like chains being drug across the attic floor, and then some banging down the stairway, would run them off. These people started telling their stories around, and pretty soon people steered clear of that old place.

The fellow that owned the place hadn't lived in his new house very long until he began to hear noises like a woman screaming over at the old house late at night. Since a panther's scream is just like this woman's, he tried not to think too much about it until one night he got curious and sat up with the front door open, waiting for the scream. Sure enough, before too long he heard it and stepped out on the front porch and looked over toward the old house. Just about where the front door was located was a light like a lantern swinging back and forth.

This old boy didn't ask any questions; he just took off running to a neighbor's on down the road. He stayed there all night. The next morning, he went back to his house, packed his belongings, and went back to his other farm. His mind-set was to never step a foot back on that place again. He got plumb desperate about what to do with the farm, so he set out to sell it all, lock, stock, and barrel.

People around there heard all these stories about it, and wanted no part of it. Some time later, a man that had heard all about this bottomland for sale came inquiring about it. Not being too superstitious and more interested in cropland, he decided to buy it. So he gave the owner a downpayment and left.

A few weeks later, he brought his wife along with some of their things and moved in. That night these people left, never to be seen in these parts again. People who saw that man later on over in his community said he wouldn't say a thing about that night.

Well, the owner still had the title and was still trying to sell it when me and these two other men were passing through there one time. We were all young gallivants and weren't scared of nothing, and said so when we heard the story. As it turned out, we went to talk to the owner and asked him if we could spend the night in that old farmhouse just to show everybody that it wasn't spooked.

The old man told us that if we could spend the night in the house, he would sell us the house and farm for $200. We all decided that it was a deal. The three of us were actually on our way back from selling the logs we had rafted down to Nashville and we were tired from the trip. So we took out for the old house to get some rest and a bite to eat.

When we got there, I remember how awful the old house looked. Well, we went inside and laid down our bed rollings. I struck a match and found an old lantern on the mantel. I lit it and we started talking about going up the steps to the loft to make sure there wasn't anything up there. I took the lantern and up the stairs we went. We looked around, but the only things we saw were dusty old spiderwebs and some dark spots on the floor over in the corner.

Satisfied, we went down the stairs, fixed us up a fire and a bite to eat, and began telling the stories we had heard about the old place. We talked until nearly one o'clock before we thought we'd try to get some sleep. None of us felt like anything was going to happen, and that we were part owners of the farm.

Well, I don't know what time it was, but it was close to daylight, when all of a sudden I woke up to the awfulest noise I ever heard. It was like a panther screaming, or a woman yelling. I woke the others up, and we grabbed our guns. We stopped breathing and started listening as hard as we could. The only thing I could hear was my heart pounding like a drum. And then, there it was just as plain as day, a big rock as big as my fist came down the chimney and landed in our fire.

We knew something was going on then. I thought it was somebody playing a prank on us, trying to scare us off. I rushed to the door and flung it open but couldn't see a blooming thing, except the pitch black dark. I told the others to come with me and we'd have ourselves a look-see. We prowled around out there in the dark for a long time, but didn't see or hear a thing. We figured that it had to be a chimney rock that fell down through the chimney because of our fire. So we had ourselves a laugh and went back inside.

Just as I closed the door, I heard it! Lo and behold, there was somebody dragging a chain across the floor of the loft, or attic. Then, all of a sudden it stopped. I was plumb scared to death! I looked at the other fellows, and their eyes were all bugged out. I whispered, "Did you hear that?"

They said, "Yeah, what do you reckon it was?"

Still not hearing anything right then, I said, "Boys, I've got to be dreaming."

They said, "No, sir. That was somebody or something dragging a chain across that loft floor."

Well, that noise began again, and we just stood there as stiff as pokers, listening. That chain then came across to about where the steps ended, stopped for a second, then came down the stairs and landed against the door.

Well, sir, we bolted out that door just like the old devil himself was after us! We ran quite a piece down the road until we were out of breath, and when we saw that nothing was after us, we set down to catch our breaths. We waited until daylight, and by that time our courage was mustered up a little. One of the fellows suggested that we go back and take a gander at what was up them steps. So we agreed to do it, then headed back. We got there and went in, but there was not a sound to be heard.

The others begged me to go open the door since I could run faster, and they'd wait at the door with guns ready. Kid-like, but being awful curious, I took the dare and opened the door. There was no chain, no nothing, at the foot of the stairs. We thought we were plumb crazy to think we had heard that chain lodge there!

Well, this boosted our courage, so we started up the steps. We had all made it to the top without anything happening, but when I stepped over a loose plank, my foot hit a chain. I like to have died! I leaped down them stairs with the others right on my heels, and out of that house we ran. And that ain't all, Bud, I ain't been back!

Joe Morrow, as told to David Morrow, Russell Springs, April 4, 1971.
Courtesy of Folklife Archives at Kentucky Library,
Western Kentucky University

Ghostly Manifestations

Jefferson County

This is something that happened in my house. There were two family members that died in my house, and one who lived there when she was murdered in Jefferson Memorial Forest. My room was her room then. One of the ladies in the family collected bells for her upstairs room.

My stepmom and I would randomly hear bells ringing upstairs after this lady passed away. We would go upstairs to look, but no one was up there. Also, the bathtub upstairs down the hall from her room would occasionally turn on, but no one was up there. And we see flashing lights in the hall going upstairs which appear to be ghosts!!

My stepmom claims that when she washes dishes, she sometimes feels a cool breeze, and when she looks up toward the fan, it isn't on.

A few years ago, some radio station had a contest asking for people to send in their stories, and the Louisville Ghost Hunters Society would come out and check out the winning story's house for any activity. Sure enough, they found activity in all the upstairs rooms, including mine.

Ashley Beckum, Jefferson Community and Technical College,
Louisville, February 2008

Ghostly Sounds of Water and Falling Tree

Logan County

When I was small, Mama and Daddy lived in a house down at Keysburg. They had to move from there. Mama said they had to move away from there. They said they couldn't sleep because they could hear water pouring at the foot of the bed. She said that it then sounded like a tree hit the house and rolled off down in the creek. You could hear the water splashing when the tree hit it.

That kept happening, so they just didn't stay there because they couldn't sleep since they kept hearing this water pouring and the tree falling. They didn't know what was making that noise, but they thought it was some kind of ghost. They couldn't figure it out because they couldn't find out what it was.

They didn't take it any longer, so they just moved away from there because they couldn't sleep in that house. Things like that did happen.

James L. Pearson, Lewisburg, March 22, 2008

Weird Old House

Logan County

When I was a little boy, we were picking strawberries, and there was an old house setting back there. You could hear somebody in that house just like somebody cooking. I said, "What is that?"

My father said, "That house is haunted."

Well, I went in there, but couldn't find a durn thing. But if you got out in front of the house, you could hear somebody rattling dishes, pans and stuff. It was interesting to hear something like that.

As a part of that, two guys got killed out on the Orendorf Mill Road. A buggy run over one guy down there and killed him. That was about a mile and a half out of town going toward Dot.

When he got killed, me and the old lady were living in a house over there when we got married. And I never seen another house like that old house. It was a carbide house. It had carbide lights in it. Carbide was in a big tank out in the yard. They'd put that carbide in, and they had water in there where it would seep and makes these lights burn. . . .

But in the morning, you could get up and you'd hear music playing out on the front porch, just as plain as anything. I mean, they was making music if you'd set there and listen to them. We thought it was ghosts making the music.

They finally tore the old house down and put a trailer out there. That was the first house I'd seen like that.

James L. Pearson, Lewisburg, March 22, 2008

Door Opening Sounds

Hardin County

The only ghost story I can tell is about myself and Roger Goad, who is originally from Monroe County. We were partners for several years in the late 1970s and early 1980s. We were embalming a body one night in this building around 1977. All at once we both heard this door open about two or three o'clock in the morning. I said, "What was that?"

He said, "I don't know."

Well, we jerked off our garb, came out and turned the lights on, and walked all around this building and didn't see anything. We never did see anything. We decided that something indeed did happen, because that door opened.

We know it opened, but we never knew what was going on.

Bob Brown, Elizabethtown, September 25, 2007

Ghostly Noises and a Man's Voice

Warren County

Around 11:00 P.M., the Internet was my only friend. My cats were lazily cuddled up in velvet fabrics left over from my last crafting session. The room was void of light; thus, the only source of light was coming from the incandescent computer screen. I jumped up at the sound of clicking, then went weirdly looking around. In doing that, I realized that the gas stove was on. When I went rushing over there to turn it off, the sound suddenly stopped. Throughout the next two days the stove continued to turn off and on by itself.

One night when I was alone again and almost asleep in my bed, I heard a voice, deep and rich. I could tell it was a man's voice. When I heard that voice, I quickly sat up in my bed, but the voice disappeared. I never knew whose voice it was.

Sara Joye, Bowling Green, May 7, 2008

Weird Ghostly Noises and Lights Years Ago

Carter County

This story is told to be the truth. Whether it is or not, only the dead know, since the generation of people who claimed it really happened have been buried now for many years. I was about eleven years old when this story was first told to me while visiting my cousin's grandmother Marie.

Marie is now about eighty-seven years old and still lives on the same property where this incident took place. She first learned of this story from her mother when she was a young girl, but only after telling her mother of the things she had seen.

It took place in rural Carter County, Kentucky, on the outskirts of Carter City. The country road leaving a state highway and ending at this farm still looks much the same today as it did when I was there as a young girl. There are a few farmhouses along this road, and Marie's farm is the last one and is at the end of the road. As you approach the property, the road is flat and straight, and it literally ends, being their driveway. The little, white framed farmhouse is located to the right of the driveway, with lots of shade trees showing their age. Straight ahead of the last footage of road is a field where the horses and cows once made their home. To the left of the road is a strip of land where they have gardened for generations. Marie still raises her own food there. Up ahead beyond the garden area in the distance is an old road that leads into some trees. The tree line goes across the entire end of the farm, with the old road being the only opening. Even then, when I first rode up and noticed the layout of the land, I noticed the old road and thought of how it looked so mystical. It's the type of view as seen in many paintings that makes you want to see what is hidden just beyond the view.

On my first trip to Grandmother Marie's, we stayed fairly close to the house, playing in the yard. We could find fun in just about anything, as well as nothing. Just getting to go spend the day with my cousin was good enough for me.

My second visit to that farm took place a couple of summers later when I was about thirteen years old. It was on a Sunday, and late enough in the summer that some of the vegetables were ready to be picked from the garden. We played in the yard most of the afternoon with the dog and some young kittens, sprayed each other with the water hose, drew drinking water from a well, and hung out in a cool cellar. I loved that place because it was remote and away from the normal routine that I was used to. Late in the evening as the hot temperatures started cooling down, we walked to the garden to join Marie while she was picking some corn. Being in the middle of the garden, I got a much better view of the old road leading into the woods that fascinated me so. I asked her where the road led to and what the land was like on the other side of the tree line. Even then, Marie was an even-paced lady with her hard work as well as her conversation. When I asked the question, she walked over to where my cousin and I were and sat down beside us on some logs that were lying along the edge of the garden. After a moment of silence, she gestured for us to sit beside her. For a second, I wondered if I should have even asked. As she started telling the story of the past, her eyes slowly drifted toward the old road and the opening in the trees. Then she described the field that lay just on the other side of the tree line. She said that it was really beautiful and the old road eventually ended when the trees all became a forest.

Many years ago the road had served as a passage to other farms and families, but over the years the land had become deserted and the trees flourished everywhere. Marie went on to tell us that when she, too, was very young she was intrigued with the road, and when she would tell her mother she was going to walk it, her mother would tell her it was probably not a good idea. After many tries of getting her mother's approval, her mother told her it would bring her bad luck. Times were hard enough and no one wanted any more hardships than they already had. Marie told us as a child, there were a couple of nights when she was playing in the front yard just after dark and she saw what she thought was a light coming from the opening in the trees. She first thought it was some sort of reflection from the moon, but after looking long and hard she could not find the moon or any reflection of the moon anywhere. She said she only experienced this twice.

Not long after that, while her mother was busy from farm chores, Marie decided to venture down the forbidden road and into the woods. She knew she could probably go there and no one would ever know. She said as she started walking toward the trees there was calmness in the air. She often took walks in other areas of the farm and enjoyed her time alone, but this time it was different. She said she passed through the trees and sure enough it opened up into a beautiful field. There were no buildings or houses, and no signs of anyone ever living beyond that field. There were birds and squirrels there, just as there are anywhere in the country. A couple of rabbits ran out in front of her, startling her just for a second. Marie walked around slowly observing her surroundings. She was looking for anything that appeared to be different, but didn't notice anything. She said the only thing she found different was the silence, the calmness of the air, and what seemed to be untouched land with magnificent beauty. Her thoughts were mixed as she walked back home.

She wondered if there was any truth in what her mother told her about having bad luck. It was hard for her to understand, since she only saw the calm and pretty land. But she remembered seeing an unexplained light on two different occasions, and knew now there really wasn't anything in that area that could have caused a reflection from the moon. For several nights after her adventure, she lay awake in bed thinking about all of this.

A few weeks later, Marie and her mother were working in the garden and she asked her mother to tell her what she knew about that place. Her mother told her the story that had been told to her. She said a member of the family that owned the farm before she moved there many years ago told her of the families that lived on the surrounding farms. The old road leading into the trees and the field had at one time been the only road passing through there. In its time, it had gone on beyond the field and a couple of miles farther to other homesteads. It was during that time that some men rode up during the night with lanterns and pulled a man out of his house and hanged him in a nearby tree. The story claims that his death was brutal, as his family watched with no defense of their own. This family had lived two farms up beyond where the field now ends and the forest begins. In time, all of the surrounding neighbors found out what had happened, but during those days people didn't have much opportunity to find out information beyond only what they actually experienced. No one ever knew who the men on the horses were and why the man they killed was their target. Families lived in fear for years thinking this may happen again, and as they died off, their children moved away, not wanting to live in that hollow. All of the surrounding property was either sold and left unattended, or set for many years with the heirs dying off as well. There were tragedies that followed throughout the lives of the surrounding families.

As Marie sat and listened to her mother, she now wondered if she did the right thing by venturing off the day she went there. Her mother went on to say that when she was very young she also saw a light at the edge of the trees where the road was. She had seen it several times but could never explain it. When she confided with a neighbor as to what she had seen, the neighbor told her the last person to live there had seen a black horse running up the road and into the area of the open trees. It was just after dark and there was a light glowing just above the saddle, but there wasn't anyone riding the horse. The neighbor said this happened several times. Marie's mother, who was a faith abiding, God-fearing mother, later went to her grave convinced of what she had seen.

After Marie's mother told her the story, she never went down that road again. Just a few years later, Marie met the love of her life. They were true companions and best friends. They had three children early in their marriage, two sons and a daughter. Marie and her husband, along with their children, stayed on the farm at her mother's request, since Marie's father had passed away and her mother knew in time the farm would be hers anyway. Marie's mother lived many more years on the farm and remained there until her death.

It didn't take long for the fate of Marie's walk down that road to haunt her. Just a couple of weeks after the birth of their third child, her husband was killed on the job where he was working. It was a freak accident that should never have happened. Marie and her mother raised her three children, working on the farm, growing their own food, raising cattle, and growing tobacco. Just after Marie's children graduated from high school, her daughter left the farm to go to college, and her two sons got married to their high school sweethearts.

The youngest son was very happy in his marriage, and a year later he and his wife had a baby girl. Three years after the baby's birth, the father was killed in a car wreck. His wife quickly remarried and Marie never got to spend much time with her granddaughter.

Marie has lived her entire life on the farm and still lives there today. She still has never ventured beyond the tree line anymore. She has experienced much heartache from her losses and has remained alone with her memories. She is a very private person and has worked hard her entire life. Even though she's nearing her nineties, she's still one of the toughest persons I know. She has a lot of knowledge of not only the land, but how to survive from the land. She still drives herself to a little country church a few miles down the road every Sunday morning. And she still drives the same car that she bought new in the early 1950s. That is the only time she leaves the farm.

Rhonda Campbell, Grayson, March 27, 2008

Strange Glowing Lights

Harlan County

Big Laurel is located in Harlan County on the north side of Pine Mountain. Around 1950, after a long illness, one of the elders of the Big Laurel community passed away. This was a loss for the community as well as his family. People from the whole area of Bledsoe came to the visitation and funeral to pay honor and show respect.

After a forty-eight-hour wake and a five-hour Pentecostal funeral, the man's weary family headed to their home for dinner and rest. As they were having supper they noticed out through the kitchen window a bright light in the cow pasture. They continued eating, but continued to wonder what it could possibly be. Someone suggested that it was probably a visitor with a flashlight coming to check on them during such a stressful time. The light never moved while they continued eating.

When dinner was over, one of the men in the family decided it was time to go see what the light was. Everyone gathered at the back kitchen door. When the man approached the light, it disappeared. He hollered back to his family, and they all said they still saw it just fine. The man walked back to the house and he, too, could see the light again. He walked back to it a second time and once again it disappeared, but everyone else at the house could still see it.

Other family members began taking turns going out to see the light, but when they got about ten feet from it, it disappeared. The strange light disappeared entirely after about an hour, and was never seen again.

This was not the first or last time mysterious lights were seen in Big Laurel. Residents claimed for many years to seeing peculiar little lights traveling on the hillsides. These lights were far too large to be fireflies. They did not twinkle, but maintained a steady glow from the time they appeared until the time they disappeared. Spectators claimed that on some nights they counted up to thirty of these glowing orbs in the mountains.

Several individuals set out to find the source of these lights. After the lights appeared one night, about five young men from the community hurried up the hillside to find an explanation for this frequent occurrence. Once in the mountains, they saw no sign of the light. When they hollered down to their friends who stayed down below, they said the lights were all still hovering and moving slowly over the hillside. These men who were searching in the mountains never saw a single light.

The lights of Big Laurel were a regular occurrence many years ago, but many say the glowing globes are now a rare occurrence. From time to time, though, they still make a mysterious appearance.

The Boggs family, as told to Darla Jackson, Big Laurel, 1981

Weird Nighttime Sounds

Trigg County

In the subconscious mind of most of the pioneers, there abode a deep and supernatural belief in the regular occurrence of supernatural events. Shortly after the turn of the century, peculiar occurrences began to be noticed in an old house in Trigg County.

It had been built before the Civil War and was the main house on a good farm, but the place could not be rented because of strange noises that terrified the residents. After retiring at night, the occupants of the house would be awakened by peculiar noises from the living room.

In this large room there was a big fireplace which required logs of considerable size. There would come a sound from this large room after they had retired for the night, like a log of wood rolling from the fireplace. When they rushed into the room nothing could be found. This continued constantly during the winter. No one could stay at the house.

The last tenants were a man and his wife, both of whom died of nervous diseases, one of them in the hospital of the insane [located in Hopkinsville].

The mystery was never solved, and after these people died the place was torn down.

Pear Newbold, as told to June Wells, Earlington, 1961. D. K. Wilgus Collection, Southern Appalachian Archives, Berea College

Ghostly Rocking Noises

Wayne County

There was this family that lived in an old house in Wayne County, Kentucky. When their first baby was born, it died after two days. After the baby died, the couple moved away because they didn't want to live in the house in which their baby had died.

About a month after they moved out, another family moved into the house. The first night they were there everyone heard something rocking upstairs. The father went upstairs to see what was making the noise. The noise was coming from the room where the baby had died that belonged to the couple that lived there first.

Whenever the father, or any of the family of the people living in the house, would approach the door, the rocking would stop. The family stood it as long as they could, then moved away. This house was never lived in again.

Charlie Coffey, as told to Foster Coffey, Owensboro, 1961. D. K. Wilgus Collection, Southern Appalachian Archives, Berea College

The Shaking Spirits

Morgan County

There used to be an old house near Moon, Kentucky, on what is called Dock's Creek. This house could not keep its occupants long at a time. They all became afraid and moved out not long after moving into it. The story goes like this:

The first occupants noticing anything strange about the house were Mr. and Mrs. Rufus Hayes. Mrs. Hayes's father had given the house to them when they got married, and they moved into the house shortly afterwards. The very first night, in the wee hours of the morning, Mrs.

Hayes woke up very frightened because she heard a rattling noise like pots and pans being banged about in the kitchen.

She woke Mr. Hayes up and he heard the noise also. They got up and lit the oil lamp and went to the kitchen door. When they reached the door everything became very quiet, but they went on into the kitchen to see if something was there. They did not find anything at all that could have been making the noise, so they went back to bed and dozed back to sleep. They woke up again with a start; there was that noise again, only louder this time. They again looked around but found nothing.

This time, they did not go back to bed, but sat down in the dining room to wait for the noise. In a little while it began again, but the Hayes did not stop to see about it this time. They ran across the road to Mrs. Hayes's father's house and spent the rest of the night there.

They went back to the house in the morning, but found nothing that could have made the noise. They lived in the house for something like a month, then departed from the house completely.

The house was rented many times, but each time the occupants heard the shaking or rattling spirits, they moved out.

After a few years of this, Mr. and Mrs. Hayes had the house torn down [around 1920], and a new one was built there in its place. The spirits were never heard in this one.

Hammie Ison, as told to Leota Sherman, Moon community, 1960.
Leonard Roberts Collection, Southern Appalachian Archives,
Berea College

Weird Creature Heard and Seen

Monroe County

A story was told to me by my grandmother about an old woman and her friend who had just started home from their vacation when they heard of a house that was said to be haunted. The woman did not believe in stories such as this, so she decided to prove that it was ridiculous. She went to the owner and asked if she might rent the house for an overnight stay.

About 5:00 P.M., the woman and her friend arrived at the huge house. After dining, they sat before the fire and talked until about 9:00 P.M., according to the story. The friend soon went to her room next door to that of the doubting woman. About midnight, they were awakened by a horrible scream. The friend ran through the old woman's room and disappeared into the street.

For a moment the old woman was inclined to follow her friend, but suddenly she was terrified to see a human hand come out of the wall and, as if by magic, shone bright until she couldn't bear to look at it. But when she again looked, it had disappeared.

My grandmother related that by dawn the old woman was so stricken with fear she could barely move. Then, seeing a horrible-looking creature that appeared to be part human and part animal coming toward her, she fled in terror through the open door.

The woman had been home only a short time when she received a letter from the owner of the old house saying that it caught fire and burned the next day. Residents who live nearby said that as the house burned they heard horrible screams and saw a strange creature, such as the one the woman and her friend had seen, rise up out of the flames and rest over the house until it burned to ashes.

Margie Shirley, as told to Gary R. Martin, Tompkinsville, 1961.
D. K. Wilgus Collection, Southern Appalachian Archives,
Berea College

The Everlasting Spring

Nelson County

Northeast of Bloomfield in a rather widely spaced area are at least five everlasting springs. The best known of these is the one just across the highway from the historic Big Spring Church. During past droughts, barrel after barrel of water have been taken from its depths, but regardless of how much it was lowered, it was replenished by the next morning. In this water has been found blind fish covered with rough growths resembling warts.

Years and years ago, so goes an old tale, a yoke of oxen, crazed by thirst, broke away from their driver and dashed madly into this spring, only to sink slowly lower and lower and become lost to sight.

Today, the bottom of the spring is covered with large heavy stones resembling cut foundation stones. These were evidently dropped in at random. The water now stands at a depth of some three feet.

On certain spots in the area bordered by these everlasting springs, there has been heard a peculiar holler rumbling or echoing sound. This would occur during a long dry season, and at late afternoon or dusk. A farmer driving a team of horses hitched to a wagon would hear not the usual sound of hoofs and iron-rimmed wheels, but a holler reverberation like that heard in passing over a bridge, only deeper and more resounding.

People wonder if the sounds are the results of there being a huge cave, or a subterranean lake, but most people think of the imprisoned spirits and of the long ago drowned oxen lowing for release.

Grace Snider, as told to Anna Ruth Burgin, Bloomfield, 1959.
D. K. Wilgus Collection, Southern Appalachian Archives,
Berea College

9

Strange Sounds, Lights, and Unexplained Events

~

Girl's Ghost Leaves Pennies

Warren County

Potter Hall, located on the campus of Western Kentucky University, is known for strange and unexplained happenings. Many people working in this building tell stories about their personal experiences of encountering the ghost of a young female who hanged herself in a ground floor dorm room, shortly after her boyfriend broke off their relationship. Today, Potter Hall houses administrative offices, and the ghost commonly known as Penny frequents every floor.

One morning, the building service attendant began her day at 4:00 A.M. by vacuuming an area of carpet in the lobby. Upon completion of her task, she noticed several pennies lined in a row on the freshly cleaned carpet. She knew she had been visited by Penny, the ghost.

Another day, an administrator on the ground floor was washing her hands after using the restroom. She heard the sound of coins hitting the tile floor. Turning around to investigate the noise, she found three pennies lying on the tile.

I, myself, working in the same office, have experienced the humor of Penny. Many times I have returned to my keyboard to find pennies wedged between the keys.

We are not sure of the young girl's name who found her demise in Potter Hall, but she is well known as "Penny," because she chooses to leave the copper coins as her trail.

Anonymous contributor, Western Kentucky University,
Bowling Green, December 28, 2007

Ghost of Van Meter Auditorium

Warren County

There was this man that was working in Van Meter on the last night of the stage production, and he fell and came down. Certain people have supposedly seen his spirit as the ghost of Van Meter. Some were staying in the building, one of whom was a boy who didn't actually believe there was such a thing as he had been told.

He stayed in the building that night. He was sleeping on the stage, and he felt a presence at two o'clock that morning. He looked up and saw a bright blue light. Because of that, they replaced a window at the back of the stage.

Another boy went up into the loft above the stage, where the ghost is supposed to stay, and he quickly dropped out of school, because he saw a light, real bright and blue. When he dropped out of school, he took psychiatric treatments.

Always it's a bright blue light that they see, along with certain other things. And there's been other strange occurrences. I talked with the janitor in Van Meter, and he told me he stayed in there one night because it was snowing really bad. He said he'd never spend the night there again because of the noises that go on there.

Sammy Lawson, as told to Nelson Graham, Meade County, January 5, 1968. Courtesy of Folklife Archives at Kentucky Library, Western Kentucky University

Insane Girl's Ghost

Scott County

There was a dormitory at Georgetown College, with four floors. And there was a timid girl who lived by herself on one of the floors. She was studying to be a nurse, and two girls that lived next to her were also studying to be nurses. Their room had light cords that hung from the ceiling.

One night the girl went out, so the two girls next to her decided to play a joke on her. They got an arm from a cadaver, and hung it on the light cord with the hand hanging down. They waited in their room for the girl to come in.

The girl came in and the light came on, but they didn't hear her scream or anything. After a few minutes, they looked into the room and saw the girl sitting in the corner, rocking the arm and taking bites from it. The girl died in an asylum shortly thereafter.

Her ghost began haunting the floor. The two girls who played the trick on her were found dead in their beds. Their hair had turned white, and their eyes were staring at the door.

After this, the girl's ghost kept appearing, so they closed the fourth floor. The girls on the third floor could hear footsteps on the floor above them. The police looked on the fourth floor, which was covered with dust. There were no footprints, but they could still hear the footsteps.

Two years later, they finally tore the dorm down because nobody would live there.

Mike Waddy, as told to Janet Linde, Louisville, March 1952. Courtesy of Folklife Archives at Kentucky Library, Western Kentucky University

Priest's Ghostly Appearance

Warren County

Rick Eubank had just gotten back from his night class at Cherry Hall. He laid down in his bed and started reading his assignment for another class. He started to get sleepy and drifted off into a nap. He then heard his door open and footsteps coming closer but dismissed it because he thought it was his roommate returning from his night class.

In a kind of daze, he saw a figure moving through his room. The figure then stood at the end of his bed and smiled down at him. Rick was not scared, and thought he was dreaming. He pinched himself several times. The figure came closer, and Rick then thought he recognized it as a priest from his home town.

Just then he heard the door open and saw his roommate once again come into the room. Rick then turned around to look again at the figure, but it was no longer there.

Rick Eubank, as told (about himself) to Jeff Mitschele, Mt. Sterling, November 28, 1970. Courtesy of Folklife Archives at Kentucky Library, Western Kentucky University

Floating Ghostly Light

Lewis County

In the early 1900s, a little girl that lived along the banks of Billchain Creek in Garrison, Kentucky, loved to play in the fields and in the creek. Her favorite summer pastime was running through the fields catching fireflies with her father's lantern. One hot summer night as she was catching fireflies, she wandered too far from home and fell into an abandoned well. She was found dead days later at the bottom of the well.

Today, local residents claim that on certain summer nights a faint light can be seen floating across the fields along the creek. Most people believe it to be the ghost of the little girl running through the fields with her lantern, still chasing fireflies.

Bryan Wright and Mary Weddington,
as told to Lacey Wright, Garrison, May 20, 2008

Mystery at the Ford Mansion

Trigg County

The old Ford Mansion in the Boyd's Hill community, near Linton, was haunted. On the other hand, Ford descendants who lived there ignored the stories of eerie lights, spooky noises, and the sounds of footsteps when it was apparent no one was there.

The mansion, a big two-story structure, stood on a hillside overlooking a valley that led to the Cumberland River only a few hundred yards away. One dark night, a neighbor riding by on a horse noticed a light behind the house—a yellowish glow that silhouetted the building against the trees in the background. It faded quickly, and suddenly a ball of light about the size of his hat bounced over the house, hit the road in front of him, then disappeared. His horse panicked, whirled, almost tossed him out of his saddle, and raced out of control back up the road toward Boyd's Hill Church.

Late one night some weeks later, while checking what he thought was a disturbance among his livestock, a neighbor who lived across the valley from the Ford place saw a glowing object going around the house, bobbing a bit as it went. Then it rose in the air and bounced seemingly along the rooftop and disappeared.

Once while visiting the Fords, a neighbor said he heard footsteps upstairs, although all those that lived there were present in the sitting room. He made no comment, neither did they as the footsteps seemed to come down the stairs and fade away.

A series of rattling noises coming from the upstairs rooms were frequently reported by those who visited the Fords, even during daylight hours. Neither was it unusual for a neighbor to report numerous sightings of the glowing yellow light, especially late at night. For some reason, the light almost always hovered near the base of the chimney outside at the south end of the house.

Rumors as to what caused the lights and noises were many. The one most accepted by those who lived in the neighborhood was that when the house was built, the original owner had included a secret compartment where he had concealed a large sum of money. Unfortunately, he had died suddenly, leaving no clue as to where his money was hidden. The noises, footsteps, and lights from a kerosene lantern were distractions while descendants looked for the hiding place. The flashing lights were explained as coming from steamboats plying the waters of nearby Cumberland River.

When land along the river was being cleared for the waters of Barkley Lake, a number of homes in the floodplain were demolished, including the Ford mansion. Report was that when the chimney was torn down, a cache of money was found. That report was quickly denied, however. Money or not, no eerie lights or mysterious noises have been seen or heard in the vicinity since.

Edison H. Thomas, Boyd's Hill, February 19, 1992.
Courtesy of Folklife Archives at Kentucky Library,
John Morgan Collection, Western Kentucky University

Ghostly Piece of Furniture

Knox County

This story has its beginning in Barbourville, Kentucky, the hometown of my wife, Pat, who was a Disney. Her grandmother, Mary Disney, died in the late-1970s. Pat's grandfather had died several years prior to that and had lived in downtown Barbourville. These Disneys were related to Walt Disney.

Back several years prior to his death, Mr. Disney bought a huge piece of furniture. Most people today still have difficulty in identifying what the piece of furniture is. One identification is that it might have been the backdrop of a bar, because it has got a lot of beveled glass, and a lot of these little shelves where you can set the bottles, glasses, and so on.

Anyway, this piece of furniture had set in Mary Disney's home for many, many years. It had accumulated a great deal of dirt and dust over the period of time. After Mary died, her daughter Marie was the executor of the estate. It got down to the point to where she had offered this big piece of furniture, which was a beautiful piece of solid oak furniture on which were all these carvings. Many think it had come from Cincinnati. It has this German influence in terms of the carving inside, or it might have come from Swiss Colony over in Laurel County. The latter would be the most likely place in which James Disney purchased it many years ago, likely in the 1920s.

Because it was such a huge piece of furniture, no one in the family could take it. So it got down to where just about everything in the house had been cleared out. They had a buyer for the house and were going to tear the house down. Pat's grandmother, Marie, tells her they have a buyer for this piece of furniture.

So, Pat talks to me and says, "Well, let's buy it; we'll do something with it. We'll get it home."

I don't know which came first, but around that same time we decided to expand the back of our house in Frankfort. In so doing, we added a family room, and we expanded our dining room. Thus, we had room to actually place this piece of furniture in there.

While it was still in Barbourville in the old house, we went by one day so that Pat could take some photographs of it. The two of us, along with her mother, were there. At the time most of the photographs were taken, I was not in the room where this piece of furniture was located.

We got the developed pictures back, and in the mirror image was a black image of a man's profile. It was very identifiable as a man. Pat had taken another photograph where her mother was sort of located off to the side. And her image was in a second photograph, but it was in color. We have never been able to figure out where the image of the male profile came from.

At the same time, some of the other photographs that Pat took then had in them what looked like a couple of beams of light going diagonal across the mirror. Likewise, we couldn't figure out where those light beams had come from. So, those photographs established what we called a ghost in this piece of furniture.

One of Pat's younger cousins, who still lives in Barbourville, had seen the photograph. When it was first shown to her, she started shaking, then said, "My gosh, that looks just like Granddaddy Jim," which was her grandfather that passed away many years ago. I couldn't relate it that way, because I never saw him.

Anyway, it was a major job to move that piece of furniture from Barbourville to our house in Frankfort. We loaded it up on a U-Haul back in the 1980s and brought it back to Frankfort and put it in our garage, then spent one afternoon cleaning it with vinegar and oil—just something to get the dirt out of it. After that, we put a light coat of clear varnish on it, then locked up the garage and left the furniture overnight.

Before I went to work the next morning, I came out to the garage just to take a look at the furniture to see if it was dry. When I went into the garage, on one of the top shelves it looked like that someone had put paint on their fingers and had run a streak across the top of one of those shelves. We couldn't figure out where that had come from. This big piece of furniture had doors on the bottom, and when I opened up those doors, on the inside of one of the doors there was a double streak of what looked like white paint.

We have since moved this piece of furniture from Frankfort to our new home in Scott County, located ten miles out of Frankfort. That's where it sits now. We have not had any experiences of any other activity of the ghost since we moved the furniture, but have often wondered where those streaks come from. I looked at the paintbrush we had used, just thinking maybe we had used an old brush, or something, that had leached out. But it was a brand new brush.

So the combination of the man's profile in the mirror in black, the streaks of light going diagonally across the beveled mirrors, and the paint strips across the top and behind the door are what this story is all about. We left the paint strips behind the door.

So, that's our story about the ghost in the piece of furniture.

Don J. Dampier, Georgetown, March 15, 2008

Old Corbin Hospital

Laurel County

A group of seniors from Whitley County High School decided they would go on a haunted goose chase. It was said by virtually everyone that no one could stay in the old Corbin Hospital for one night, but these students were up to the task. Their names were Sue Sizemore, Patricia Hatcher, Ryan Fox, Brandon Pratt, and of course, me, Lisa Tennison.

We headed out about 4:00 P.M. on a Friday night, which was Halloween. We pulled up in Patricia's Blazer. We took with us flashlights, batteries, and other things we would need. We got there around 7:30 P.M.

After we got in there, we decided to look around. Everything was very old and torn apart, so we decided to go into Psycho Hall, where all the nuts stayed. It was getting darker as we entered the room. There were curtains and beds around the nuts. We heard a loud noise, and Ryan said, "Hey, guys, did you see that over there?"

I said, "No, it's your imagination. Let's go back and set up places to lie down and talk."

When we all got back to the main entrance area, we heard loud screams and people crying out, "Help me, please. Someone help me."

When we heard that, we just figured it was someone from school trying to scare us, so we blew it off. Then, about 9:30 that night, we decided to go lie down and wait the night out. All of a sudden, Sue started screaming, "What's wrong? Something scratched the hell out of me."

She turned around, and we could see scratch marks down her back. We all decided it was time for us to leave. We packed up and were headed out the door when a loud creepy voice said to us, "Never come back."

Well, we left and never did go back. That was in 2005–06, which was our senior year. We didn't go back, and never will go back to the old Corbin Hospital.

The story behind that old hospital is that a patient was in the room where the nuts stayed, then went crazy and started killing people. He killed twenty-three people, then took his own life, according to the way people tell it. So we call it a legend.

Lisa Tennison, Corbin/Bowling Green, May 19, 2008

The Old Garder House

Fleming County

On Black Diamond Road in Fleming County, there stands an old fallen-in house, and beside of it is a dirt lane covered with a thick forest. To neighborhood kids this is a place where you never wander past the gates, especially after dark. As a child, I was told the story of two coon hunters who were not from around this area, and who mistakenly went hunting out there one night. It was a full moon, and Jed and Bill had decided to come see their cousin down in Kentucky. While there, they decided to go hunting with some dogs that they had bought.

They drove around for a little while, then trying to decide on a place to go hunting, they decided they would just stop at the gate that they had seen. There were no signs stating no hunting, or nothing, so they went in.

For the first three hours or so, it was good hunting as they had caught three coons. Then, when hunting, their dogs started acting weird, whining around, and stuff. They looked up, saw the old house, and saw a light moving. They saw it again and saw that it was an old woman with a lantern in her hand. Therefore, they walked to the house because they thought that someone was there. They knocked, the door fell open and they saw their coon dogs were dead. The dogs' heads had been cut off and were hanging from the ceiling. Then they started hearing something out in the woods running back and forth. The next thing they knew, they saw this man. Then they headed back to the fence just as fast as they could go. As they got closer to the fence, Jed heard a loud howling. When he finally reached the fence, he saw that Bill did not make it.

Jed went to get the police and they searched the grounds that day but found nothing, not even a speck of blood. None of the officers, not even Jed, would go back in after dusk. Would you?

Kennetha Stout, Lewis County High School, May 20, 2008

Talking Ghosts

Logan County

We lived in Russellville on the Nashville Road in a little white house across the road that used to be there. Me and [name omitted] and [name omitted] would be in bed, and Mama and them would be across the hall in their room. And there would be what we thought were people sitting at a table and talking. We heard them talking about going to the store and everything. When we heard them, we'd get up and look, but there wouldn't be anybody there. We'd go back to bed, and they'd start up again!

I didn't know what to think, but you could hear them people just as plain as anything, just sitting there and talking.

Linda Parsley, Lewisburg, March 22, 2008

The Rocking Cradle

Pike County

When my mother was a young woman, she had one child at a time. She and her husband lived in a house with their young baby. One day, Mother put her sleeping baby in the cradle and left the room to work in another part of the house. She heard the cradle rock and thought the baby was awake. She went to check on the baby in the cradle and found that the baby was asleep.

Every time she put the baby in that cradle and left it, she heard it rock. But she never saw anything.

In that same house, Mother would hear footsteps that sounded like a lot of people walking to the door. When she went to open the door, no one was there, but the footsteps were going to another door. She never saw anyone.

Mother became so frightened she took her baby and sat in the barn door until Father got home from work. They soon moved away from that house.

Orethia Miller, as told by Lola Stanley, location unspecified, 1971.
Leonard Roberts Collection, Southern Appalachian Archives,
Berea College

Preacher's Haunted House

Breathitt County

On Lick Branch in Breathitt County there lived a preacher by the name of Bob Herald. He lived in a house said to be haunted. At this house there were many strange things happening. People all around had heard of this and would come from miles around to try to see these strange things.

Greenberry and Charlie Turner went one night when it was said the swing was supposed to start swinging and the chair was to start rocking, and the door was said to come open of its own accord. Greenberry Turner sat in the rocking chair, but it didn't rock, and Charlie Turner sat in the swing, and it didn't swing.

The next night, two more members of the same family went to see what they could find out. They rode horseback to this man's house. Along up in the night, the doors flew open, the chair began to rock, and the swing began to swing. These two men got so scared that they ran off and left their mules hitched to the fence all night. The next morning they went back and got them.

The very next day, Bob Herald moved away, and the house burned that night. Old people of this community said that one of his boys shot at the sun ball and cursed the Lord, then the devil gave him power to do those strange acts.

This is true as told by Greenberry Turner, who visited this house.

Roscoe and Verlie Turner, Avawam, 1956.
Leonard Roberts Collection, Southern Appalachian Archives,
Berea College

The House of Mystery

Pike County

One day we were getting ready to move to a new place over on Road Creek. Everyone said, "Now Lennie, you'd better stay here; that place is supposed to have spooks."

But I just said, "But I don't care; we're going to move anyway."

Well, the next day, Alta Fay and I moved. We listened for just any kind of noise, and two nights later the latch on the kitchen door turned.

Well, we had an old bobtailed cat in the house and it was in the kitchen, so we didn't think much of what happened. Next night, we heard somebody try to bust the door down and I screamed, "Lord have mercy, what is it?"

Phil said, "Ah, it's just old Bob wanting in."

Two weeks later, we were sitting in front of the coal fire and heard a cane or a stick going upstairs. We heard that noise three times and we thought it meant that Phil would get killed. So, the next morning Phil stayed home and we went back to Mother's for a couple of days.

Later, I heard something and said, "Phil, don't you hear something?" and he said, "No."

Then the doorknob started turning again and many times we'd go to the door, but nobody was there. That night the men were out fox hunting and I heard another noise that sounded like someone was pouring something out upstairs. Then about that time I heard something at the front door. I went to the door, but nobody was there, and it was during the wintertime and it got dark early. Stupid me, I went out and looked under the steps and didn't see anything, so when I went back to the house I looked to see what time it was, and it was 5:30. Phil came home at 10:00 that night and didn't more than get in bed when the knocking started again over on or under the big grandfather clock, and that lasted from 10:00 until the alarm stopped. And the longer we stayed, the worser it got. After that, Phil went outside and later came back in and said, "Lennie, awhile ago I saw something that looked like smoke coming down the road toward me and I came on into the house."

Three months and two weeks later, Alta Fay saw a ball of fire coming toward her, so she ran. A couple of days after that we moved. I never did know the reason why we heard all those sounds, but someone told me that when the house was first built, the daughter let an old man go without food for two weeks at a time and he died of starvation. Sometimes the people living there before would go out, and when they came back in the table would be set.

They say the old house was torn down and a brick house was built, but that didn't help any at all; the noises kept on. The man that bought the house from us sold out and moved.

If someone had told me this, I probably wouldn't have believed them, but I lived there and I know, and nobody could make me doubt that I didn't hear those noises.

Lennie Ratliff, as told to Roberta Dunn, location unspecified, 1970. Leonard Roberts Collection, Southern Appalachian Archives, Berea College

Ghostly Noises

Barren County

Alexander and Helen Beatty lived in Barren County between Nobob and Summer Shade. They had three kids at that time, Guy, Roy, and Alta. What I'm about to describe took place in 1894.

In the middle of the night, they were awakened by a noise originating outside of the house. It sounded like someone was scraping the sides of the house. . . . The sounds would change locations and go to another side of the house. At times it sounded as if a plank was torn off, one end placed on the ground, and the other end held by hand with a foot placed in the middle and forcibly flapped to the ground.

This sound persisted so long and was so intense that the two boys sleeping upstairs woke up and were frightened. They came downstairs where their parents were. Alex wanted to go outside, but Helen insisted that he not go. He had no gun or other defense weapon. There was no phone and no close neighbors.

The noise lasted so long that they came almost to the end of their tolerance. Finally, the sound moved to the roof of the house. It sounded like the shingles were being torn off and thrown through the air with such speed that the ghostly sound was produced by shingles.

At last, Helen became so upset that she cried out, "All God fearing people would be home in bed at this time of night." Following this, there was a long scraping sound over one side of the house and it disappeared. The next morning, they examined the house, and the roof and shingles were intact.

Alex bored a large hole in one side of his weatherboarded house and borrowed a shotgun from his brother-in-law, but there was no repeat visit. There was never an explanation of the ghostlike phenomenon.

Dr. Oren A. Beatty, Louisville, March 23, 1992. Courtesy of Folklife Archives at Kentucky Library, John Morgan Collection, Western Kentucky University

The Ringing Bell

Allen County

This took place around 1958 on my grandfather's farm in Allen County. The farm is located on Highway 98, near Fountain Run. The house was an old two-story log house that had been weatherboarded before my grandfather bought the farm around 1940. It was said to have been built during slave times and according to my grandparents had always been haunted.

My grandfather, who was Fred M. Stinson, was widely known all over Allen County as a merchant and peddler. He became terminally ill around 1956. He spent his last year of life bedridden. In order for us to hear him when he needed something, my aunt bought a school bell for my grandmother to keep by his bedside. He rang it when he needed something. Grandfather passed away in 1957. After his funeral, Grandma took the bell and put it in the chest of drawers located in the bedroom in which Grandpa died. The bell was forgotten about.

Late one Saturday night Grandma was away visiting relatives. That left my mother, myself, my sister Brenda, and a girlfriend of hers that was spending the night with her. All the doors were securely locked, as usual. My mother and I were asleep in the upstairs bedroom, and my sister and her girlfriend were in the living room, sitting on the bed and talking. All of a sudden, around midnight, my sister and her friend both heard the faint ringing of a bell. It kept getting louder and louder. They could tell it was coming from my grandfather's bedroom and was getting closer to them. There was a door that led to the hallway, located right by the headboard of the bed. The door was closed. The sound of the bell came right up to the door. My sister was not afraid of anything, so she loaded the gun. The bell kept ringing and ringing. Her girlfriend was so scared that I don't believe she ever returned to the farmhouse.

The sound of the bell then moved to the outside of the living room window and continued to ring. At that point, I believe my sister really got scared, as she and her friend came upstairs where we were. The sound of the bell then moved into the living room and started ringing at the foot of the stairs. It even rang louder and louder. My sister then woke my mother up, and at the instant she woke up the ringing ceased. My mother never did hear the bell ringing.

They were all too frightened to go back down the stairs that night. The next day, my mother went into Grandfather's bedroom and the bell was still in the same chest of drawers in which it had been placed after he died. She also checked all the doors, and they were all still securely locked.

The next day, we took the bell back to my aunt's house. I can't explain it, but it never did hurt anyone. We never did see the bell, just heard it.

About a year passed and the bell experience was history, or so we thought. Again on a Saturday night, when my grandmother was away visiting, the second occurrence took place. My cousin Ernie was visiting me for the weekend. All doors were locked and secured. My mother and sister were sleeping upstairs, and me and Ernie were sleeping in the living room in the big comfortable featherbed. Absolutely no one else was in the house. It was very late, around midnight I suppose. Ernie and myself had been talking and joking, as kids will do. We both had just dozed off to sleep when we heard the bell ringing in my grandfather's room. It woke us both at the same time. The bell did not ring loud, nor did it ring long, but it was coming from Grandpa's room. It rang just long enough to scare both of us kids to death. We both covered up our heads and did not move until morning.

When we told my mother of that experience the next morning, her eyes grew wide and there was a look of fear on her face, as well as my sister's. It seemed only to happen when we had company and Grandma Harriett was away visiting. Granny never did hear the bell to my knowledge.

As I sit here tonight writing this story, cold chills are running all over me.

Danny R. Clark, Bowling Green, February 1992.
Courtesy of Folklife Archives at Kentucky Library,
John Morgan Collection, Western Kentucky University

Weird Noises in the Wilson House

Land between the Lakes

Dad was asked if his father or mother ever had a disturbing experience while they lived in the Wilson house. He said, "The only time that Dad or Mother, either one of them, ever knew of anything suspicious was the night when there was some sort of an entertainment at the school-house and all of them went to the entertainment, with the exception of Mother and Dad.

"They were sitting in the room by the fire, and were picking cotton. Back then you had to pick the seed out of the cotton with your fingers. Well, so they were sitting there when they heard the hall door open.

"It was a huge double door and it had a latch at the top, with a chain that came down to where it would be an easy reach for any of them. When you opened that door, the chain would bang on the door, and rattle, and that sort of thing.

"First they heard dogs barking, just barking, barking, barking. Finally, they quit barking. Well, just after they stopped barking there was a click of the latch on the hall door. The door opened and the chain rattled and someone stepped inside, shut the door, stood there for a second. Then you could hear steps, one, two, three, four, five, six, seven, just about long enough to walk into the boys' bedroom and then turn around and walk back into the hall.

"It just happened that George and others were cutting timber that day, and a chip hit George in the eye. When he left for the entertainment that night, he had a bandage over his eye with some slippery elm bark or something on his eye in order to ease the pain. So they jumped to the conclusion right away that George's eye had gotten to hurting him, so he had to come home. When he got home, Dad got up and went to the door and called for George, but he didn't answer. Well, Dad went back, took the lamp off the table and went to the boys' room, and also the front room, but no one was there. Then he went upstairs and went through the rooms up there. Since he had just left Mother in there still picking cotton by the fireside, when he got back to her, he said that he hadn't found anybody. He said he guessed that maybe it was just the cat. Mother said, 'It couldn't have been the cat. The cat was lying by the fireplace, had been, all the time.'

"So, they didn't know. They had no explanation for it and never did have. But both of them agreed on the noises that they heard—the rattling of the chain, the barking of the dogs before the chain rattled, and the footsteps. That's the only unexplainable thing that ever happened in all the time they lived there, which was a number of years."

Catherine Dycus, as told by her father, Hampton, Virginia, February 15, 1992. Courtesy of Folklife Archives at Kentucky Library, John Morgan Collection, Western Kentucky University

Ghostly Music Sounds

Montgomery County

This story was handed down to Rick Eubanks, as told by Mrs. Francis Kern. In his words: "Mrs. Kern was a churchgoing, God-fearing woman. She had just had a baby, and three weeks later it came down with pneumonia. They kept the child upstairs in a crib, in a room of its own.

"The entire family was downstairs when they started hearing organ music playing a song they all knew, 'God Will Take Care of You.' As soon as the music stopped, they went upstairs to check on the baby. They found him in his crib dead.

"They could never explain the music because there was no radio in the house, and the nearest house was about two miles away."

Jeff Mitschele, as told by Rick Eubanks, Mt. Sterling, November 28, 1970. Courtesy of Folklife Archives at Kentucky Library, Western Kentucky University

Ghostly Mandolin

Graves County

Several years ago, I lost my mandolin and I started looking for it. I searched all day through the house from the basement all the way up to the upstairs area. And I didn't have any luck finding it, but after I went to bed and fell asleep, I was awakened by the music of my mandolin. So I got up and took my flashlight and started trying to find out who was playing the music.

I went upstairs, where the music was louder, and started searching there. Then I thought of the attic and went over to it. I started to lift the board off of the attic door and then the music suddenly stopped. When I looked inside the attic door, guess what I found?

There was my mandolin laying there all by itself without a bit of dust on it. I don't know how it got there without me knowing about it, but I ain't been back up there since.

Joe Deaton, as told to William Deaton, Mayfield, 1972. Courtesy of Folklife Archives at Kentucky Library, Western Kentucky University

Haint Story

Adair County

My daddy and mother, and two or three of us brothers and sisters, had been to church. That was back when I was about five years old and we used coal oil lights. It was in the summertime and was dark when we come around in sight of the house. Well, lights were shining out the window just as bright as you can imagine.

My dad thought the house was on fire, so he spurred up the mules and he got us to the front gate. Just as soon as we got there, he jumped out of the wagon and run into the house. It was just as dark as midnight when he looked in because there was no light. And there was no other person around, because that was way out in the country.

There wasn't any way anything could cause a light in that house, but we saw that light in the window. Now, that's a "haint story."

James Keltner, as told to Glenn E. Groebli, Columbia, 1971. Courtesy of Folklife Archives at Kentucky Library, Western Kentucky University

Little Boy's Ghost

Edmonson County

The family that lived in this old haunted house could hear things there during the night. They left there and then we moved into it. When Daddy would be away at work, we'd get a little boy to come stay with us [as a ghost].

We could hear things like a door slamming, and there was a coffin shop close to our house. They made one casket, and you could hear something like someone beating on solid wood. It would knock three times, then stop.

A man was going to work for us one day, and he was to be at our place the next morning. We heard a noise at the door, and we thought it was him coming to work, so we woke Daddy up. He got up and went to the door, but there wasn't nobody there. It was dark. We went all the way around the house with a light, but couldn't find anybody.

We started thinking the reason the house had those noises was because a boy was killed upstairs.

Bertha Houchin, as told to Gary Wyatt, Chalybeate community, 1972. Courtesy of Folklife Archives at Kentucky Library, Western Kentucky University

Ghostly Noises in House

Martin County

Once upon a time, a family of renters were coming along and saw an empty house that they wanted to rent. The owner of the house told them the house was haunted, and no one would live there more than one night. The father told the owner that he and his family weren't afraid of anything; they still wanted to live in the house. The owner told them to go ahead and live there and he wouldn't charge them anything for it.

The father and his girls moved part of their furniture into the house, and while their father went back to his other home to get another load of furniture, he got a boy to stay with his girls to keep them from getting scared.

The girls and the boy went to bed about dark and lay there until they heard a noise up in the loft. It was a big barrel full of cans rolling back and forth until finally it came down the stairs and scared all of them. When that happened, the boy jumped in bed with the girls and then they heard an awful moaning, groaning sound coming from the loft. Then they heard it coming down the stairs with its heavy feet dragging. It came on down and lay before the fire for the rest of the night. While it was resting, it groaned the whole night through.

The next morning when the father returned with another load of furniture for the house, the girls told him that there wasn't any use to unload it, because they weren't going to stay in that house. They told him about the barrel rolling back and forth and down the stairs, and the groaning haint that stayed there all night.

The father began to make fun of them, then all at once he began to hear banjos, fiddles, and guitars making music around his head, and he got so scared he and his entire family ran away, never to return to that haunted house again.

Floyd Horne, location unspecified, 1959. Leonard Roberts Collection,
Southern Appalachian Archives, Berea College

The Ghost Who Loved Her Hat

Allen County

This also happened at the old house [described above] once owned by my grandparents in Allen County. I can vividly remember my cousin Cornelia was visiting the farm for the summer, as she did many times. Late one night, while sleeping upstairs, this happened to her. First of all, let me say there was an old black lady's hat that hung over one of the beds in the upstairs bedroom. It was a Sunday hat, I suppose.

Anyhow, my cousin Cornelia was sleeping in this upstairs bed that the hat hung over. Late one night, when everyone else was asleep, Cornelia recalls that she had just dozed off when all of a sudden she felt something tugging at one of her toes. She finally awoke enough to notice that there was an old, gray-haired lady standing at the foot of her bed. The old lady was staring right at her, and simply appeared to be a mist or vapor. Cornelia could distinguish that it had the form of an old woman, with facial features and all. It was very vivid. The old lady moved around the foot of the bed and walked right up the side of the bed. Needless to say, Cornelia was too frightened to move. The old lady then reached over the headboard of the bed and took the old hat down and placed it on her head. She then sat down on the side of the bed, almost touching Cornelia. After a few moments, the old lady stood up, hung the hat back over the headboard, smiled, then vanished into thin air.

Cornelia recalls that the old lady seemed to be a friendly spirit and meant no harm. She had a very pleasant look on her face. That old hat had belonged to one of my mother's grandmothers that had passed away many years before. Cornelia did not tell us about this experience until many years after it happened. I guess it frightened her too much.

In concluding this story, we moved away from the old farmhouse in 1961, but Grandmother still owned the farm. She rented the house, once, to a young couple, but they did not stay there long. They told Grandmother the reason they moved is that they kept hearing strange noises in the old house. They would not stay there!

Danny R. Clark, Bowling Green, February 1992. Courtesy of Folklife Archives at Kentucky Library, John Morgan Collection, Western Kentucky University

Cold Spots in Basement

Nelson County

There is an old house on a hill in Bardstown that is haunted. Many years ago, a doctor and his wife lived there. It may not be true, but is said that one night the doctor killed his wife and children and buried them in the basement. A few days later, the doctor killed himself.

Nobody has lived in this house since that happened. The police won't even patrol it. There are strange, bright lights that move around in the house. You can even hear music coming from the doctor's piano, and there are cold spots in the basement where he buried his family.

One night, me and some guys went to this old house, parked the car, got out to go look in the house. We were walking toward the house and saw these strange lights moving around in one of the windows.

I wanted to go inside the house, but some of the guys chickened out when we saw these lights. The lights went out after a few minutes.

Mark Bradden, as told to Janet Linde, Louisville, December 1949.
Courtesy of Folklife Museum at Kentucky Library,
Western Kentucky University

A Whispering Ghost

Jefferson County

I was spending the night with a friend, and we slept together in the same bed. I felt someone lean right down to my ear and whisper "Lois." I even felt its breath, and I then jerked around so quickly that no one could have had time to even lie back down.

I asked my friend the next morning about what I experienced, and she told me that she did not do it. Well, believe it or not, she told me the same thing had happened to her a couple of times while she was sleeping alone.

Lois Osborne, as told to Rhonda Halgash, Louisville,
January 3, 1951. Courtesy of Folklife Archives at Kentucky Library,
Western Kentucky University

Ghostly Footsteps

Jefferson County

One day, Mrs. Bowman was down in the basement and her husband had just left the house to go get something. She was just doing her everyday thing, like she was accustomed to doing. She heard the front door open, so she thought it was her husband. She also heard footsteps walking across the floor, then called out to her husband, but he didn't answer back.

Then she went upstairs to find out what it was, but there was nobody there.

Rosemary Wimsatt, as told to Donna Sue Smith, Louisville,
November 11, 1972. Courtesy of Folklife Archives at Kentucky Library,
Western Kentucky University

Best Friend's Haunted Trailer

Whitley County

Me and my friends, Denise Evans, Myra Evans, and my cousin Rebecca Taylor, were all watching that Ring movie, but instead of the phone ringing, something else really weird happened. On Halloween, about a week after the movie, it was raining like cats and dogs. It was raining that bad. All of a sudden a big noise came from the front door. We watched a little, then opened the door.

On the screen door was a big wet spot in the shape of a circle, and glasses started breaking. Also, one of the rings Denise had lost rolled out into the floor and stopped. We watched a knife rise above the counter, then fell onto the floor standing straight up.

It was crazy and we were scared.

About two months later, the trailer burned to the ground, and we didn't know why. Even the cops and the fire department didn't know. We never knew the story about this trailer, but we always said it was haunted.

Lisa Tennison, Corbin/Bowling Green, May 26, 2008

Ghost in the Blue House

Whitley County

When I was about six years old, me and my brother Ray Tennison, and my granny, Wilma Moore, lived in a blue house toward Candatown. One night, I heard Granny cry out loud. I was little, so I went in there to see what was wrong with her. But she wasn't in her bed, so I started to cry. Then I heard Granny say, "Lisa, please help me." That is what happened that night.

Years later, I asked her what happened while I was asleep that night. She said, "Something was trying to pull me down under the bed, like it was the devil or something. It got me to the floor, then it stopped when you started to cry."

That is why we moved away from that house.

Come to find out, people were burned to death in that house, but no one found their bodies until two weeks later. So, me and my brother Ray always said there is a ghost in the blue house, so never go there. We haven't been back there since then.

Lisa Tennison, Corbin/Bowling Green, May 26, 2008

10

LEGENDS AND FOLKTALES

~

Girl Sticks Butcher Knife in Grave

Monroe County

There was just a bunch a-having a party at a girl's home one night. They just was making a bet, you know, what each one would be afraid to do. There was a graveyard right close by this girl's home and some of the other girls and boys told her that they'd bet she wouldn't go to that graveyard. And she said she would go, that she wasn't afraid! So, one of them told her, says, "Well, you take this butcher knife," says, "You stick it in a certain grave over there," says, "We'll know then that you've been there."

This girl, she took the butcher knife and when she knelt down to stick it in that grave, she caught her skirt, and when she started to raise up, naturally that butcher knife held her skirt down and scared her so bad, why, she died. So that's where they found her, was there by that grave.

Willie Montell, Rock Bridge, 1964

Preacher Obtains a Treasure

Kenton County

Preachers have a lot of hard work to do—welcome the living in, baptizing them, seeing the dead out of this world by baptizing them, keeping people on the straight and narrow, and involved in full time work. But one of the hardest things this preacher had to do was to exorcise this ghost.

People came and said it just wasn't right for a good house to go un-occupied with so many people needing shelter. They said terrible things went on in this house, so the preacher went to the house to investigate what was happening. He took along with him his trusty Bible that went wherever he went. He went on into the house just as the sun was going down, and built a fire in a fine stone chimney. It was a nice house that had three or four rooms and a cellar in it. He sat in a chair and put the Bible on the table next to him and he read it as he rocked, and the fire was keeping him warm. Everything was just fine until midnight when he heard a voice say, "OoooooooooOoooooOOOK!"

Directly after hearing that blood-curdling scream, he started hearing Tnnk! Tnnk! Tnnk! Tnnk!—something coming up the cellar steps. The door from his room to the cellar creaked open, and that was too much for the preacher. He jumped up and yelled, "Who's there? What do you want?" Then the door closed back on him. The preacher looked down at his Bible that had fallen off his lap onto the floor, and he felt a little ashamed. He was a preacher and he had such little faith. He picked up his Bible and sat back down in the chair and started to read. That's when he heard Tnnk. Tnnk. Tnnk. Tnnk.

This time the preacher was ready, so he said, "In the name of the Father, the Son, and the Holy Ghost, who are you and what do you want?" That's when something started taking shape in the doorway. The preacher thought it looked like the shape of a young woman. She started drifting across the floor to where that preacher was. As she got closer, he realized it wasn't just the shape of a good-looking young woman, but it was the shape of a person that had been buried for some time.

As she got closer, he realized some of her flesh was decaying. He could smell a newly turned dirt smell. And it came right up to him and grabbed him by his lapels. The preacher quavered, "What do you want?" Then her voice came to him like the wind blowing. "Whhhhhaaaaatttt I want is for you to givvvvve me a good Chrisssstian burrrrrial."

He said, "Where will I find your bones?"

"Diggg innnn theee celllllar, and you'lllllllll finddddddd myyyy bonnnnnneees. Puttt thisss inn theeee colllllectionnn platttee SSS-Sunday."

The preacher didn't know if it was a dream or an apparition, but when he kind of woke up from his trance, in the palm of his hand was a little finger bone. He put it in his pocket and took his ladder down to that cellar, one step at a time until he came to the dirt floor in the cellar. He saw a pick and a shovel, and he took the pick and swung it and it hit something hard. He loosed up the dirt with a shovel. And in the first shovelful he unearthed something white and glistening. In each shovelful he found another bone. He took off his coat and laid these bones on it until he had every bone of that young woman.

He took the bones and gave them a good Christian funeral in the church cemetery. He buried every bone except that little bone she had given him. He forgot all about that until he went to preach his sermon. He put his hand in his coat pocket and struck that bone, then he remembered what that voice had told him. And he'd never preached such a sermon before. It was about justice and divine retribution. He had everybody shaking in their pew.

When it was time to take up the collection, he started out himself with a dollar bill, and underneath his dollar bill he put that little finger bone. As he sent that collection basket all through the congregation, there was a young man who didn't come to church very often, but he was there that Sunday. When he put his contribution in the collection basket, and brought his hand back out, he brought something with it, then yelled, "Get it off, get it off, get it off of me. Get it off of me. I killed her. Get it off of me."

They grabbed the fellow and took him down to the sheriff. That finger bone wouldn't come off of his hand until he had signed his confession.

The preacher had one more job to do. He went back to that house and sat down. At midnight that voice came back to him again and said, "Dig under the hearth rock, and you'll find the goldddd." He pulled it back, but there was just dirt. He used his hands this time and he unearthed a chest. There was gold in it!!

They built a new Sunday School building and named it after that woman who was in the house.

Greg Jowaisas, as told to Linda K. Adams, Covington, June 10, 1990. Courtesy of Folklife Archives at Kentucky Library, John Morgan Collection, Western Kentucky University

Pretending to Be Headless

Harlan County

At an outcropping of a mine in Harlan County, a headless man would appear every so often. The miners were very much disturbed and afraid.

One night two men were working overtime while waiting for some equipment to be brought in, so they laid down to rest. All at once the headless man appeared and they jumped up and started running, with the headless man flopping behind them. They came upon an entrance that had been abandoned, and saw a light.

They ran in and there was a group of men with bottles and jugs. The headless man came in and got out of his disguise, telling the men the coast was clear. When he saw the two men, he wanted to know what they were going to do with them. The two men told him they would not tell on him.

These bootleggers were making whiskey and selling it to some of the miners. The headless man did this act so that they could keep the way cleared in order to deliver the whiskey.

John Blalock, as told to Patricia Ann Lewis, Cumberland, 1960.
D. K. Wilgus Collection, Southern Appalachian Archives,
Berea College

The Bad Ghost

Metcalfe County

One day a ghost named Charles went to a haunted house. There he found a bad ghost, a ghost that was bloody and dirty. The bad ghost never did take a bath. When Ghost Charles got there, the bad ghost always chased him. Eventually, the bad ghost fell into a hole. Charles heard him yelling, and at that point in time the bad ghost died and he never chased Charles again.

Jimmy Welsh, as told to teacher Kay Harbison, Summer Shade, 1969

Ghostly Daughter Kills Parents

Metcalfe County

There was a woman who lived in a house with her parents. She was sick, and finally died. Before she died, she told her parents that if there were such a thing as coming back to life, she would.

Well, every night at midnight, when it was raining, she would come back and go upstairs and sleep in her bed. Her father heard her coming up the steps one night. He saw her but could not touch her. She always laughed when he tried to get her. They put different kinds of locks on the door, but she would just break it and walk on in.

Finally, one night when she came in, her mother and father saw her. They told her that she was dead, but she always told them she would get them back. She then followed them to the room where she died, then murdered both of them, screaming aloud, "I told you I would get you back. You will never see me again."

Rita Young, as told to teacher Kay Harbison, Summer Shade, 1969

Ghostly Man Rides Horseback

Monroe County

My daddy always said that there used to be a haunted house close to Mt. Herman in Monroe County. He said that when anyone would pass by that old house on a mule or horse, there would be a man that would hop up behind you and ride on down the road holding on to you, then would suddenly disappear into the air.

Jackie Kingrey, as told to teacher Kay Harbison, Summer Shade, 1969

Ghost with One Black Eye

Metcalfe County

One day, this husband and father said to his family, "Are there any potatoes?"

His wife said, "I do not know, but I will go and see." She went down to look for the potatoes, and she saw a ghost. The ghost said, "I am the ghost with the one black eye," then he went on to eat her.

When she did not come back, her husband, said, "I am going down there to see about her." When he got there, he saw a ghost with one black eye. Well, the ghost proceeded to eat him also.

When the father did not come back, one child said, "I am going down there." When he got down there, he saw this ghost. The ghost then said, "I am the ghost with one black eye," then went on to eat the child, too.

When the child did not return to the house, a second child said, "I am going down there, too." When he got there, the ghost said, "I am the ghost with the one black eye."

The child said to the ghost, "If you don't stop bothering us, especially me, you will soon have two black eyes!"

Deborah Deweese, as told to teacher Kay Harbison, Summer Shade, 1969

Stealing Sheep

Metcalfe County

I heard this story about these fellers that were stealing sheep. They was stealing sheep and they'd meet at the cemetery and divide them up. Well, people would see them, then get to talking about a ghost that was in the cemetery.

One feller said that he wasn't afraid of ghosts, so he said he was going to see about what was happening. When he got to the cemetery, he didn't see them because it was so very dark, but these two fellers were there dividing up the sheep they had been stealing.

One of the thieves came into the cemetery with a sheep on his back, then the other thief went up to him and said, "Is he lean, or is he fat?"

The thief with the sheep on his back said, "Fat or lean, take him."

Well, this feller that wasn't afraid of ghosts thought they was talking about him, so he took off running as hard as he could go!

Clayton Barrett, as told to teacher Kay Harbison,
Summer Shade, September 3, 1968

Dividing Up the Dead

Monroe County

This is a ghost story my mother told me when I was small. She said there was three men and they were going home. They had a father who was crippled and had been in a wheelchair for several years. Well, these boys started home, but they had to go through an old graveyard.

When they got to the graveyard, there was this walnut tree there. There was some men gathering walnuts, so they would say, "You take this one, and I'll take that one."

These three boys just stood there and listened, but they soon got scared and started running home. When they got home, they went to their crippled father and said, "God is up there at the graveyard dividing up the people, so come on let's go listen to them."

Their father said, "I can't walk."

They said, "Come on, we'll help you."

So they took him up to the gate at the cemetery, and they was standing there listening to these men say, "You take this one, and I'll take that one." Soon, one of these men said, "Wait a minute, I left one at the gate."

The old crippled man jumped out of his wheelchair and outran them all. He thought they were talking about him!

Florence Graves, Tompkinsville, 1975

Lydia's Lost Soul

Harlan County

John Smith had just turned twenty-one, and was living the life! He was almost done with college, and had a good job in his hometown, Cumberland, Kentucky. The only thing he needed now was someone to settle down with. He was tired of all his party days.

It was getting dark outside, and John began to leave his work for the day, and it seemed that the rain had set in to stay for awhile. He decided to ride around for a little while because he wasn't ready to go home for the night. Suddenly, he noticed a beautiful girl with long blonde hair walking slowly through the rain. He stopped to ask if she needed a ride, and she politely said, "No, thanks." When he arrived home that night, he found that he couldn't get the girl off his mind.

A few days later, John was driving through the same area when he noticed the girl walking again. This time he knew that he wouldn't let her get away from him, so he pulled his car to the side of the road and ran to catch up with her. They walked and talked for a few hours until the girl finally said she had to go.

"Wait, you never told me your name," John said.

"Lydia," she replied.

"But when can I see you again?" asked John.

"I just don't think it would be a good idea," Lydia replied, then suddenly ran out of his sight.

John didn't know what to do, as he really liked Lydia. The next morning, he awakened to the phone ringing and the sound of Lydia's voice saying that she wanted to see him again. John was ecstatic. They made plans to go to dinner later that night. As soon as John arrived at her house, she came running to the car. They went to the steak house and ate, then spent the rest of the night talking and driving around. When they arrived back at her house, it was a little cold outside, so John gave her his jacket and walked her to the door.

As soon as he awoke the next morning, John was thinking about Lydia. Considering that he had left his jacket with her, he decided that this would be a good excuse to go and see her. When he got to her house, he went to the door and knocked three times. As he began to leave, a woman came to the door and slowly opened it. "Can I help you?" she asked.

"I'm here to see Lydia," John replied.

"Lydia?" she questioned. "She died three years ago."

"You must be mistaken," John said. "I was with her all night last night, and this is where I picked her up. The reason I came back is to get my jacket that she kept."

"Follow me," said the woman.

They walked for a few minutes until they came upon a small cemetery. She pointed to the small grave with a picture of Lydia. "This can't be right," John said, as he looked to the left and noticed his jacket lying over her grave.

Selina King, as told to Rikki Gaines, Cumberland, March 26, 2008

Hilltop Ghost

Russell and Casey Counties

There was a bus driver with a busload of people driving on Highway 80 during a dark, rainy night. The driver stopped at the bottom of the hill to pick up this woman who was by herself. It was really spooky looking that night.

The driver started up the hill and happened to look into his rearview mirror and saw that the bus was completely empty, except for the last woman he had picked up. See, before he picked her up, the bus was completely full of people.

By this time, he was really scared when he got to the top of the hill. When he got up there, the woman wanted to get off the bus, so he let her get off. He then looked into his rearview mirror and noticed the bus was full of people again.

It is said that, even today, you can be driving your car on Highway 80 on the Russell-Casey county line, and this woman will get in the car with you, then get out at the top of the hill.

Phillip Bolin, as told to Mike Brannik, Russellville, May 1972.
Courtesy of Folklife Archives at Kentucky Library,
Western Kentucky University

Scared Man Jumps Out of Grave

Logan County

There was a cemetery in a very remote section in the northern part of the county in which a grave had been dug and left open overnight for a burial the next day. Later that night, an old drunk man came wandering through the graveyard, and he accidentally fell into the open grave. He tried and tried to get out but could never do it.

While he was still in there, half asleep, another man fell into the same grave. The drunk man said, "You can't get out of this grave."

Scared to death, the other fellow leaped out of the grave, then yelled back, "Yes, I can, and yes, I did!!!"

Hazel Fleming, Lewisburg, December 13, 2007

Boyfriend's Ghostly Scratches

Fleming County

This boy and girl were out together one night and they ran out of gas. He decided to go get some gas, so he told her to lay down in the car on the floorboard. . . . He told her not to open the door for anything, no matter who was there.

So after she'd been there for a couple of hours, she heard this scratching on the doors. She laid there and just kept hearing it, and hearing it, for the rest of the night. And when it got to be daylight, a policeman came to the car, knocked on the window and told her who he was. She finally opened the door and the policeman told her to get out of the car and to go with them, but not look back.

She started walking, and had to walk quite a distance to the police cruiser. Just as she was getting into the police car, she decided to just look back anyway. She did this just to see why she shouldn't look back.

When she does look back, there's her boyfriend hanging from a tree over the roof of the car. So it was his fingernails scraping all night long, scraping the top of the car all night long.

Lee Goodpaster, as told to Leslie Calk, Fleminsburg, date unknown.
Courtesy of Folklife Archives at Kentucky Library,
Western Kentucky University

Murdered Baby's Ghost

Jefferson County

This story is about Crybaby Lane off U.S. 42, near Skylight, Kentucky. It is about this girl that got pregnant a long time ago. The guy wouldn't marry her, but she decided to have the baby anyway.

Well, after she had the baby, she didn't like it. So, one night she went out to this lane and took an old pair of scissors and stabbed the baby, then threw it in the bushes. A few weeks later, the girl couldn't live with her conscience, so she went and told the police what she had done. They went out to the lane to find the body, but never could find it.

The baby somehow lived, and grew up out there with the animals. It is said that if you go out there at night, you can hear it crying. It is still alive!

Bruce Turner, as told to Janet Linde, Louisville, May 1951.
Courtesy of Folklife Archives at Kentucky Library,
Western Kentucky University

A Ghost Didn't Do It

Logan County

There was this ghost that was supposed to have an axe to hit people in the nerve in the back of the neck to kill them. Two girls lived in this house, and they'd heard about the ghost, but they weren't scared or anything. They had an outhouse, and one of them went out to use the bathroom. She said sarcastically that if she weren't back in five minutes to come and get her. She went out and came back in a minute.

Later her roommate went out, but she didn't come back. So the other girl got worried and went out to see about her friend, and she'd been locked in the outhouse. She'd been scared and died of fright while clawing on the door. When they found her, the cause of death was that she'd been hit on the back of the neck and was getting paralyzed.

Kathy DeShazer, as told to Mary Kirk DeShazer, Russellville, January 2, 1970. Courtesy of Folklife Archives at Kentucky Library, Western Kentucky University

Victim Imagined He Saw Mountains

Pulaski County

One time there was this young man that was being initiated into a club. He had to spend the night alone in a big old haunted house was out in the country. It wasn't around here though, because there ain't no place around here that is that spooky.

Anyway, he was there by himself when he saw these mountains with snow on the top of them. He kept thinking that if he could only reach those mountains, he would be safe. He struggled all night, but finally reached them.

The next morning when his buddies came to get him, they found his head lying on the front porch floor, and his body hanging over a broken window. What had happened, as near as they could figure, he had been so scared that he just went crazy.

The mountains he thought he saw was just a broken window. It was broken real jagged, and frost was on top of the jags. When he had got to what he thought was the mountains, he just flung himself over the top. The glass was so cold and sharp it just cut his head off.

Lloyd T. Godby, as told to Janice Simmons, Science Hill, November 1972. Courtesy of Folklife Archives at Kentucky Library, Western Kentucky University

Rapping Spirit Counts Money

Edmonson County

Here's a story about a man with some money. He came to Aunt Martha because he just wanted to see for himself if she could call the rapping spirit. He told Aunt Martha this because he had so much money in his pocket. He wanted her to call the rapping spirit and ask it to rap on the table the number of times that added up to the amount of money in his pocket. He told her he would give her all the money if she could do it.

So Aunt Martha called the spirit. It started rapping on the table and rapped for a hundred times. So when the man pulled out the money, sure enough he had one hundred dollars in his pocket.

He tried to give the money to Aunt Martha, but she wouldn't take it.

Bertha Houchin, as told to Gary Watt, Chalybeate community, 1972.
Courtesy of Folklife Archives at Kentucky Library,
Western Kentucky University

No Women Allowed

Harlan County

As a child, Jonathan Jackson had enjoyed fairy tales even more than most children usually did. He spent many summers with his grandpa in a small mining camp in Lynch, Kentucky.

The old miners would sit in front of the general store and would tell some tall tales. The longer they would talk, the more outrageous the tales would become. Everyone would just laugh, and each miner would try to top the other miner's story. One day a miner they called Crazy Bill started to tell about a beautiful girl named Mary. But then Jonathan's grandpa leaned over the heads of the other miners and smacked him. "Don't you dare say her name again, you fool," he shouted. "You know what will happen to those miners still working down below." Crazy Bill looked around and whispered, "I'm sorry; my God, I'm sorry. I forgot."

Jonathan didn't know what was going on. He looked at his grandpa and begged him to tell the story. But Grandpa shook his head no, then said, "There was too much danger for those miners working below."

Then Grandpa said to Jonathan, "Son, don't you ever say that girl's name three times in a row, because if you do, those miners will die."

Jonathan started to laugh at his grandpa because he just couldn't believe a yarn like that one. Grandpa looked at him and said, "Boy, you'd better believe."

"Okay Grandpa, whatever you say." Then Jonathan asks his grandpa if he could tell the story without saying her name.

Grandpa looked at him for a minute before replying, "Okay, you may be old enough to hear this." Then Grandpa began to tell this tale about a young girl who came here one summer to visit her grandparents. She was quite beautiful with long blonde hair and deep blue eyes. All the miners wanted her. But she would have nothing to do with any of them. She always told them that she was too young to date. Most of the young men respected her wishes and left her alone, all except Dan, who fell in love with her the moment he laid eyes on her. Dan brought her flowers and candy. He showered her with gifts, and finally she agreed to go out on a date with him. Dan was overwhelmed with joy, and told her he would take her anywhere she wanted to go.

So on the night of their date, he went to pick her up. What Dan didn't know is that she had heard the rumor that no women were allowed in the coal mines. They all said it was bad luck for a woman to go underground. If a woman should enter a mine, death was sure to follow. She thought that was the funniest thing she had ever heard. She made up her mind to prove this old wives tale was wrong. Besides that, no one told her where she could go, or what she could do.

Dan arrived to pick up his date, and couldn't believe his eyes when he saw her standing there wearing pants! No respectable girl would wear those in public; maybe in the city, but certainly not here. He wonders where he could take her. Her grandma asked her where in the world she thought she was going wearing pants.

Mary laughed and said, "Oh, Grandma, just down to the fishing hole to have a picnic."

Grandma made Dan promise to not take her anywhere else. He made that promise to her and even said, "I cross my heart and hope to die if I do."

Dan didn't know what was ahead of him when he made that promise. As soon as they walked out through the door, he asked Mary where she really wanted to go. She told him that she would like to go down to the mines. He said, "No way. If I take you down there, it will be bad luck for all."

She looked at him and started to beg, "Please, do this for me."

How in the world was he going to turn her down, because he loved her. So he took her into the mine. They walked inside the mine for about a mile, but he kept telling her not to touch anything.

"Don't be silly," she called out. "Nothing is going to happen. I'll prove it to you." Then she reached out and started to shake a support beam. When he saw what she was doing, Dan screamed, "Don't do it."

It was too late; the roof started to cave in. The very last thing he saw was a huge rock crashing onto her head, blood running down her body. Dan ran for his life, and the next thing he knew, the miners found him on the ground. He was calling Mary's name and pointing into the mines. The miners tried to find her, but they couldn't. She must have fallen into one of the deeper shafts.

Dan had to go to Grandma and explain to her what had happened, but she took one look at him and screamed, "Don't you tell me she's dead!"

Tears ran down her face as Dan told her what happened. "I don't want to hear her name ever spoken again," she screamed out, "and if you say it more than twice, death will be on your heads. I curse you all." She looked at Dan and said, "You can go too, for you will never live to see another day."

She was right, for Dan took his own life the next day. Yet he knew before he took his last breath, the town would be cursed.

When all that happened, Jonathan jumped up and screamed, "Bloody Mary, Bloody Mary, Bloody Mary." He just laughed until he cried. He couldn't believe that everyone thought this was a true tale.

The next day, a huge explosion shook the mountains and sixteen miners lost their lives. Jonathan was sent home and never allowed to return. To this date, no one else has ever said her name, and no one else has ever died in the mines at Lynch, because the mines were closed shortly afterwards.

Since the mines have closed down, I wonder what would happen if I said her name, "Bloody Mary"?

Hey, I just said it once, for I still have to live here.

Nancy Johnson, as told to her son, Jack Johnson, March 30, 2008

The Woman with the Lantern

Martin County

Once upon a time there was a woman who lived in a house by herself. She couldn't keep the door shut, so every night a little woman with a lantern on her head would come and go all through the house, and would motion for this lady that lived there to follow her. The little woman wouldn't do it, but one night she decided to follow her, because she didn't think whoever it was would hurt her.

When the little woman with the lantern came and motioned her to follow her to the cellar, she did. When they got there, the woman with the lantern motioned for her to start digging on the dirt floor. She began to scratch the dirt away, and when she had done this she had uncovered an oven lid. It was full of gold, and when she turned around the woman with the lantern had disappeared, never to be seen again.

Josie Branham, as told to Floyd Horne, Inez, 1961.
Leonard Roberts Collection, Southern Appalachian Archives,
Berea College

Water in Woman's Grave

Russell County

This story was told to me by two of my cousins who both saw the same thing. This story is about an old woman who was run over by a car. She had lived on top of a hill, the second house from the graveyard in which she was buried. Late one evening about two weeks after her funeral, the girl who lived in the house next to the graveyard was standing on the porch when she saw the old woman walking up the hill wearing the white dress she had been buried in. She walked right past the porch and on into the graveyard.

The girl ran into the house and told her folks, but they thought she was joking. The next evening about 10 P.M., her brother was on the porch when he saw the old woman coming up the hill. He said, "In the name of the Father, the Son, and the Holy Ghost, what do you want?"

The old woman answered, "There is some water in my grave. Will you ask someone to get it out so I can rest in peace?"

The next morning, the boy went to the old woman's son and he dug her up. Sure enough, water was standing in the grave. Then they buried her in a dry place, and no one has ever seen her again.

Glen Blair, as told to Ruth Creech, location unspecified, 1959. Leonard Roberts Collection, Southern Appalachian Archives, Berea College

Ghostly Knitting

Lawrence County

Three years ago a plane crashed in Blackberry Hollow near Richardson, here in Lawrence County. After searching all day by helicopter, the plane was finally found. Because of the terrain, there was only one way to get the wreckage out, and that was by using my father's logging equipment.

After salvaging the plane, the relatives of the passengers took the motor and a few other articles. The wrecked plane was given to my father as scrap iron. Because he didn't have enough junk at that time to make a trip to Ashland, he stored the plane on a lot near the barn where renters could watch it.

Naturally interested, one of the sons of the renters was nosing around the plane and found some knitting that one of the women passengers must have been working on. After looking at it, he naturally just dropped it on the ground and went on looking at the plane. The next morning, on his way to do the chores, he noticed the knitting was gone.

He looked around and found it in the exact place where he found it the day before. This time he took it behind the barn and laid it up on the fence. It stayed there all day, but the next morning when he checked, the cloth was back where he had first found it.

Buddy Hinkle, as told to Isaac Hinkle, Richardson, November 1973. Courtesy of Folklife Archives at Kentucky Library, Western Kentucky University

Tree Bark Wouldn't Grow

Lawrence County

Across the river in Richardson there is a farm that was once owned by Jim Akers. He lived there until he was killed by someone trying to rob him one night.

After the robber had taken all he wanted, he took Jim outside, or maybe Jim had gotten away and had run outside. Anyway, the robber shot him and left him to die, but the bullet didn't kill Jim instantly. So Jim tried to get up on his feet by holding on to a tree. While trying to get up, he tore some bark off the tree and was still holding it when he was found dead the next day.

The place on the tree where the bark was torn off can still be seen because bark would never grow over it again.

Lafe S. Hinkle, as told to Isaac Hinkle, location unspecified, November 1973. Courtesy of Folklife Archives at Kentucky Library, Western Kentucky University

Disappearing Woman

Unidentified County

My grandfather was working on the roads for the W.P.A., and had to ride to work on a horse. Late one afternoon, a woman stopped him on the road and asked him for a ride. The minute the woman got on the horse, it took off as fast as it could go, and the woman was squeezing my grandfather as tightly as possible.

When they got to a stream they had to cross, Grandfather slowed the horse down and found the woman had disappeared. He never saw her again after that.

Rebecca Combs, as told to Rhonda Halgash, Louisville, December 4, 1950. Courtesy of Folklife Archives at Kentucky Library, Western Kentucky University

Scary Clawing and Screaming

Barren County

My boyfriend and I went parking on this little road that leads right down to the edge of Barren River. We parked in a little clearing where there were no trees, but all around there were trees. The car was a convertible, and after we got in the backseat we heard a clawing on the roof. I thought it was my boyfriend playing a joke on me, but when I told him to stop, he said he wasn't doing it.

198 Tales of Kentucky Ghosts

Then the scratching got louder, and my boyfriend got in the front seat and locked the doors. Then he got out his gun and tried to start the car, but it wouldn't start. Finally it did start, and when we pulled out to leave we heard an inhuman and a nonanimal scream or groan. When we heard all this, we backed up to see if it were a person. We didn't see anything, but the scream went up again. When that happened, we took off, and the scream didn't stop until we got out of those woods.

Later, we went back there with two other guys with us, and the same thing happened again. Well, I won't ever go back there again!

Terry Ann Talley, as told to Rhonda Halgash, Horse Cave,
August 5, 1952. Courtesy of Folklife Archives at Kentucky Library,
Western Kentucky University

Old Man and the Flowers

Jefferson County

There was this Boy Scout troop that camped out in old mansions in the woods. A story going around at this time that said an old man lived in this house and came out during a full moon to place flowers on the grave of his dead wife. When he put the flowers on her grave, she would come up and kiss him. This was the only thing that kept him alive. Therefore the scouts decided to explore the old house and go see if any of this was true.

One night when there was a full moon, they walked over there. When they got there they saw the old man going toward a grave, then heard a startling scream. Three of the scouts ran off, but one stayed. He watched the old man put the flowers on the grave. The scout knew that the others wouldn't believe him if he didn't get something to prove what he saw, so he grabbed the flowers and ran.

The old man took out after him, but couldn't catch up with him. The boy ran into his tent and quickly got into his sleeping bag. A little later, the old man stood at the tent where the four boys were located, with a knife in his hand. He looked at the four boys in the tent but couldn't decide who had taken the flowers. He then said, "He who shakes tonight with fear will die here."

He then went down and looked at each boy, and when he came to the boy that had taken the flowers, the boy jumped up and ran toward the entrance of the tent. The old man reached out and slit the boy's back, and a little later he died.

The old man disappeared into the woods, never to be seen again.

Buddy Walters, as told to Mike Brannik, Louisville, May 1972.
Courtesy of Folklife Archives at Kentucky Library,
Western Kentucky University

Murder at the Mall

Warren County

The ghost story I have heard about in Kentucky takes place at the Greenwood Mall in Bowling Green. It all started in 1996 when a man was found dead in a pickup truck parked in the rear parking lot at the mall. The truck was stolen, and the man was never identified. His cause of death was never determined.

People say that if you park your car in this spot and leave it there overnight, you will see a man lying in it dead. When security is called to remove the man, he is gone. Also, there is an oil spot in the shape of a face that never washes off or fades after all these years.

The police call him "The Sleeper." They say that when they call it in, "It's a sleeper again."

Tommie Cissell, Jefferson Community and Technical College,
Louisville, February 2008

Advice from a Ghostlike Woman

Logan County

My cousins lived along the Kentucky-Tennessee state line in southern Logan County, and their home was very close to this old house. The boys said, "There's money in the wall in that house there." People used to hide money that way. Well, them boys went up there to that house to try to get that money, and they could see snakes coming out after them.

They said they couldn't get that money, so they went to a fortune teller, who acted like a ghost woman when she raised her hands and told them, "You boys had better leave that money alone. If you get it, you won't ever be able to spend it. So, you can't get that money, because they didn't intend for you to get it."

My cousin said they did leave the money alone. Things like that happened back then.

I'd like to get hold of a ghost like that. I wouldn't be afraid of it because I'd like to talk to them!

James L. Pearson, Lewisburg, March 22, 2008

The Tragedy of Old Man McLewis

Knox County

John Riley was walking home late one evening. He had stayed at his friend's house way too long. His pocket watch chimed 11:00 P.M., when he realized he was next to the old McLewis homestead. Like his grandfather, Herman McLewis came to Kentucky searching for gold. But unlike his grandfather, he found it. In 1878, Herman McLewis became the richest man in three states. Scottish by birth, Herman took him a bride and built a big house on the biggest hill around.

Everything seemed to go well for several years, and the McLewis couple had two darling sons, Isaiah and Marc, both of whom looked like their mother, Susan Johnson McLewis. She was the town judge's daughter and his only child. It was believed she was a devout Christian woman, loving mother, and faithful wife.

One evening Herman, after three days of busy meetings, came home to surprise his family. When he got there, he found his wife with another man. Outraged by the fact she was unfaithful to him, Herman shot her lover in the stomach. Then he began to chop him up with an axe. Horrified, Susan tried to stop her husband, but she couldn't.

Herman asked her, "Why are you doing this to me?"

Her reply sent chills down his spine. She said, "I never loved you; I married you for your money."

Outraged, he began to swing an axe and killed his wife. When he killed her, he cried out in anger and sorrow. Then he took the oil lamp from the nightstand by the bed and smashed it on the floor. Instantly, the room went up in flames.

Isaiah McLewis woke up smelling the smoke. He ran to his parents' bedroom and, seeing the flames, he went to the nursery to get Marc.

Isaiah didn't wait for anything after that. He ran to the Riley homestead. John Riley was his father's best friend.

After the flames were gone, and the fire was out, the only two figures you could see was Herman holding the body of his wife as he was burned alive.

Now, even after forty years, on May 6 you can still smell the smoke and hear Old Man McLewis's ghost cry in pain in the night air, pleading for forgiveness. Isaiah and Marc were placed with family members back in Scotland, never to be heard from again.

John Riley looked at his watch again, and it was 11:30 P.M. He knew he had spent too much time there. Without hesitation, he broke into a full run toward home just as the crying began.

Kaci Collins, Barbourville, April 10, 2008

The Gambling Vikings

Greenup County

There were a couple of men who had been out drinking one evening. Of course, they had too much to drink, so they started walking home. However, on their way home it started raining. About that same time, these two men found a cave and went inside. When they entered, they saw three men sitting and playing poker.

The biggest man in there, who was a Viking, asked these two men to sit down and join them in their game. They all started playing poker, and as the game went on, the Viking got low on money. Well, all he had left was a bag of old money from the 1600s. He was so sure he would win the game, he bet the bag of money. He ended up losing the bag of money to one of the men he had invited to play.

When he told this man that he had to have his money back, the winner just laughed at him and never gave the money back to the Viking. That's when the Viking got very angry at the man and then pulled out a gun and killed him. The other man that had come with the man that had been killed ran to get the sheriff.

When the sheriff arrived, he found the man dead, but he was still holding the bag of money tightly in his hands. However, the Vikings were gone. Upon inspection of the money that was in the bag, the sheriff found it to be very old money from the 1600s. They also searched everywhere hoping to find the Vikings, but never found them.

I've heard that years ago Vikings had settled in the South Shore region. Some say the Viking with the money bag was one of their descendants. However, with the circumstances being as they were, most people believe it was a ghost from the 1600 era.

The Vikings were never seen again after that murder.

Charles Vaughan, as told to Joanna Friend, Ashland, date unspecified

Hog's Ghost That Wasn't

Morgan County

This story was told to me by Sanford Kelly. He was fifteen years old when the story took place. He is now sixty-two years old. This happened on Paint Creek near Relief. Now, Mr. Kelly lives on Spaws Creek in Morgan County, just out of West Liberty. Mr. Kelly is a fiddler, just about the best fiddler I've ever heard in Morgan County. He said he found his first fiddle in a trash can in Cincinnati, Ohio, and taught himself to play.

Some boys and I had been down in the cliffs of Paint Creek to swim. We came back as far as Joe Hill's on the way home. Now, Joe had an old banger [banjo] and I could play a little, so I stopped to play a little while. The boys had gone on home, and before I knew it I had played on that old banger until it was dark. Well, I had to go home anyway.

I started home and I was kindly scared, too. On the way home I had to pass the old Coldiron graveyard. Lots of people had talked about seeing things by that graveyard and I was really scared.

My brother Charlie had an old pistol and I had slipped it out and brought it with me. I was so scared as I got near that graveyard I got my pistol out and had it ready if I did see something. The graveyard was located just above the road, and there was a fence right on top of the bank. I had just reached the edge of the fence when I heard a rustling in the weeds. I looked up and saw something white going up and down. I looked at it awhile to see what it would do. It just stayed there. So I got a little braver and decided to shoot. So I cocked the pistol and shot four or five times. Then, whatever it was went back up the hill. I took off and ran the whole two miles to my home.

Next day, my mother fixed up some eggs for me to take to the store to trade for a pound of coffee and ten pounds of salt. Just as I started to walk into the store, I heard someone say, "Somebody did me a good turn last night; they shot one of my hogs all to pieces. I have to get back home and take care of it before it spoils."

I went on into the store and found that it was Will Coldiron doing the talking. This solved the problem of the ghost. I found out at once what I had shot!

Nell C. Adkins, location unspecified, 1960. Leonard Roberts Collection, Southern Appalachian Archives, Berea College

Ghostly Noises and Secret Tunnels

Caldwell County

Just outside the city limits of Princeton stands a big old deserted mansion. The mansion stands on a dark, lonely hill grown up with weeds that give it the picture of weirdness. The overgrown path leads one to a door with creaking hinges.

As one ascends the old steps, the loose boards groan with the weight of one's footsteps. The dark mysterious stairs wind to the sky, and one can see the cobwebs and crawling insects that live in the old house. The furniture, covered with white, gives a ghostly appearance to the eyes. The old clock, now run down with the years, stands on the dust-coated mantel. The drip, drip of the faucet in the kitchen rings like an alarm bell in the dense quietness of the night. The night cries of the animals float in through the windows and sends chills up one's spine. As one proceeds farther up the stairs and into the hall, a weird cry is heard. The wind blowing through the broken window sounds like the cries of a tormented child.

Beneath the house are secret tunnels and passages that provide flight after a crime of evil has been committed. In this old dark, deserted house, on a dark stormy night these secret tunnels were used by the owner of the mansion.

Early in the evening, a gay party was in progress. The leading members of Princeton were present to celebrate a new industry which had come to Princeton. Women there were dressed gaily and were truly enjoying themselves. The men were congregated in the library discussing the new industry and its possibilities.

As the evening went by, everyone pretty well got drunk. One by one the guests began to leave. Finally, all but a few of the men had left. They were discussing politics. The discussion became very heated between the host and one of the guests. It finally broke into a fist fight. The guest drew a knife and went for the host. They fought for a few minutes, then as the other guests tried to separate them, the host slipped into one of the secret tunnels.

When everyone finally quieted down, they noticed the host was gone, but didn't know how or where. The police were called in, but they could never find any clues, or any of the secret tunnels. To this day, this man has never been seen again. No one knows where he disappeared to, or even if he is dead or alive.

The people of Princeton were shocked by this experience, so no one ever goes near the mansion for fear the host may appear. There are many tales of his appearing around the house in the night, but he always disappears when one tries to move closer. Whatever really became of this man, no one may ever know.

Margaret Schwartz, Henderson, 1957. D. K. Wilgus Collection,
Southern Appalachian Archives, Berea College

Ghost That Got Scared

Warren County

On Halloween night I went to my backyard and monsters began jumping out at me. I was so scared my heart jumped out of my chest, and I fainted. I wanted to hit them with a shovel, but most of all I wanted Mommy. I called out to her, and she came out to me just as fast as she could. Believe it or not, Mommy had a shovel in her hand. She hit those monsters with it, and it made me feel so good I thought it was funny.

It wasn't long until I heard a creaking sound coming from the backyard door. I went to see what it was I heard, and believe it or not, it was a ghost that jumped out at me.

Mommy heard me scream and she came running to me with the shovel. When she yelled "Boo" at that ghost, it ran away as fast as it could!

Hannah Neighbors, Bowling Green, November 6, 2007

Little Girl in Agony

Cumberland County

I was five years old when I heard this story told by my sister, Carol Young, about what took place in this old house. It is said that a nice little girl found a scary mask in an old house here in Burkesville. For an unknown reason, she put the mask on her face but couldn't get it off. While it was still on her face, she turned into a wicked, evil girl, all because of the mask.

She ran and hid in a room and never came out. People say you can still hear her agonizing, horrible screams during the night, yelling out, "Please get this mask off of me."

That scared me so much, I wouldn't ever go into that house.

Doc Young, as told to Noah Young, Burkesville, September 23, 2007

Three Boys Went Insane

Jefferson County

This happened six or seven years ago. Me and these three boys were walking down the street one night, and we saw this light in the house. It was a greenish light, so we started talking and trying to figure out what it was. So we started placing bets, like guys do, as to which of us was the bravest.

We finally talked one of the three guys into going up in the house to investigate the light. He went in the house, and had been gone a long time when we heard a scream. We went running into the house to check on him, then about two weeks later, he went insane. So, they put him away.

The next year, we were walking past that house again, and there was a green light on again. Two weeks later, another of the boys went insane.

That happened about three years ago, then for a year and a half to two years, nothing happened. Later on, me and the last of the three guys was walking past the house, and two weeks later he also went insane.

And so tonight, I have just come back from the house. For the past couple of hours, I've been feeling strange. So maybe it's my turn to go insane. [If I do, I'm going to grab you and yell out, "Boo! Boo! Boo!"]

Dennis Elzey, as told to Donna Sue Smith, Louisville, October 28, 1972. Courtesy of Folklife Archives at Kentucky Library, Western Kentucky University

Index of Stories by County

CPSIA information can be obtained
at www.ICGtesting.com
Printed in the USA
BVOW03s1145271217
503794BV00001B/11/P